GW00645392

Freeing Mussolini!

To Raquel for her love and patience

Freeing Mussolini!

Dismantling the Skorzeny Myth in the Gran Sasso Raid

ÓSCAR GONZÁLEZ LÓPEZ

Pen & Sword
MILITARY

AN IMPRINT OF PEN & SWORD BOOKS LTD.
YORKSHIRE - PHILADELPHIA

First published in 2015 by Galland Books as *Liberad a Mussolini*!

First published in Great Britain in 2018 by
Pen & Sword Military
An imprint of
Pen & Sword Books Ltd
Yorkshire - Philadelphia

ISBN 978 1 52671 997 3

A CIP catalogue record for this book is
available from the British Library.

Typeset by Aura Technology and Software Services, India
Printed and bound in India
By Replika Press Pvt. Ltd.

Pen & Sword Books Ltd incorporates the Imprints of Pen & Sword Books Archaeology, Atlas, Aviation, Battleground, Discovery, Family History, History, Maritime, Military, Naval, Politics, Railways, Select, Transport, True Crime, Fiction, Frontline Books, Leo Cooper, Praetorian Press, Seaforth Publishing, Wharncliffe and White Owl.

For a complete list of Pen & Sword titles please contact

PEN & SWORD BOOKS LIMITED
47 Church Street, Barnsley, South Yorkshire, S70 2AS, England
E-mail: enquiries@pen-and-sword.co.uk
Website: www.pen-and-sword.co.uk

or

PEN AND SWORD BOOKS
1950 Lawrence Rd, Havertown, PA 19083, USA
E-mail: Uspen-and-sword@casematepublishers.com
Website: www.penandswordbooks.com

Contents

Acknowledgements

This investigation would not have been possible without the contribution of many people, especially those who participated in the events narrated here. I gratefully acknowledge that I have been a privileged witness, gathering and articulating the testimonies of Bernd Bosshammer, Gerhard Opel, Herman Wollter, Hans Joachim Kurth, Erich Czeka, Toni Schneiders, Karl Ziegler, Richard Kloes and Nicolás Hoelscher, all of whom have already passed away. I would especially like to thank the Hoelscher family for all their help, and whose kindness and interest have been my main motivations.

Eric Queen, Stijn David and Jürg Herzig have loaned photographic material from their archives. Prosper Keating's suggestions for the choice of pictures were also invaluable. Professor Marco Patricelli provided me with important references, enabling me to frame my work correctly. Likewise, having the help and advice of the great historian, Arrigo Pettaco was a real privilege.

Barbara Mors-Stammler added very valuable information, as well as material that belonged to her father, Harald Mors. In the same way, I was able to enjoy the invaluable help of Christof Freiherr von Berlepsch, Ligia von Kayser, Eberhard Reichelt (+), Elli Czeka (+), Heinz Bliss (+), Kurt Engelmann, Arnold Wesenberg and Ian Tannahill. The assistance of Jesús Otxoa, Óscar Alonso and Julio Pedro del Molino was of great help for the writing of this work. My sincere thanks to all of them.

Óscar González López

Introduction

'THERE IS NO HERO OF THE GRAN SASSO, BECAUSE IN THE
GRAN SASSO THERE WERE NO HEROES'
(Harald Mors, Il Tempo Abruzzo, 10 September 1993)

During the night of 11-12 September I was informed that the Allies did not
intend to keep me alive (...). It was 2 pm when I saw the first glider landing,
later others landed successively; then groups of men advanced towards the
building, determined to eliminate any resistance. The guards that watched
me didn't understand what was happening and didn't shoot. It all lasted five
minutes. The undertaking, exponent of the organisation, the initiative and
spirit of the Germans, will be remembered in the history of the war. As time
goes by it will become legendary.

With these prophetic words, Mussolini himself described the intrepid operation
that set him free from his captors in the Hotel Campo Imperatore. Ever since the
king had ordered his arrest, following his destitution by the Great Fascist Council in

Benito Mussolini and Adolf Hitler
in an Italian propaganda postcard
from 1938. Five years later, *il Duce*
fell into disgrace.

July, Mussolini had become a precious cargo for Badoglio, who was determined to offer him over to the Allies in a gesture that would accompany his capitulation and would also reaffirm his intention of not continuing the war on the side of Hitler's Germany.

The afternoon of 12 September 1943 will go down in the history of the Second World War. Some people have defined the operation as the best command action of the entire war, and even Churchill himself did not spare any praise: as soon as the liberation of *il Duce* was known, he said to the House of Commons, 'Knowing that *il Duce* was hidden in a safe place and that the Government of Badoglio was committed to handing him over to the Allies, a daring attack, completely beyond all foresight, prevented this from happening.' The operation was a complete military success. In a war that Germany was irretrievably losing, as it bled on all fronts, Nazi propaganda was in need of a spectacular and triumphant action and

Mussolini leaving the Hotel Campo Imperatore after being freed by German paratroopers. Behind him is Inspector Giuseppe Gueli.(B)

seized on the opportunity to endorse the event, even creating a fake liberator: Otto Skorzeny. On 14 September it was reported that the operation to free Mussolini 'had been prepared by a special SS commando, led by an eminent Austrian SS-Hauptsturmführer from the SD Security Service'.

The real protagonists, the Fallschirmjäger (paratroopers) from I./FJR 7, were relegated to the background and their pretensions of getting a fair and correct appraisal of the facts were dramatically silenced. This work aims to reconstruct the operation carried out in the Gran Sasso based on testimonies from the legitimate protagonists: the Fallschirmjäger.

With this purpose, inspiration has been found in the main bibliographic references that have appeared since the end of the war. The contempt for the official version among the paratroopers gained ground from 1950. We have also used - and this is what makes this work somewhat new - the direct testimonies of nine men who took part in Mussolini's rescue. This collaboration is what makes the Gran Sasso raid become a 'living historical' event, capable of being reconstructed and reinterpreted.

Nevertheless, we have chosen the path of objectivity, the separation of ideologies and emotions, aware that we are studying the delicate pages of history.

Generic assault badge with Assmann marking. (COG)

We recognise the rising value that every event takes on over time and a serene distance from the facts allows us to illuminate them in a fairer light. Likewise, we pay heed to the great philosopher Ortega, who said that 'Each person is the best history book'. Having these direct memories from nine of the participants in the mission is a privilege for a lover of history, and this research would not have been possible without them.

1. Mussolini on board the F1-156 that flew him out of Gran Sasso. (B)

2. The friendship between Hitler and Mussolini was certified following the operation, after the former ordered the release of his dear, Italian ally. (CLM)

The Operation Begins

On 24 July 1943, fourteen days after the start of the Allied invasion of Sicily, the Italian Grand Council of Fascism met for the first time since 1939. The following morning, a vote of no confidence was passed by an absolute majority requesting that although Mussolini was not to be completely removed from power, the king would now take control of the army for the first time since Italy entered the war on 10 June 1940.

This decision is historically significant because it gave the monarch the motive to remove Mussolini, whose downfall had been prepared through a coup d'etat inspired and raised by the military and those close to the monarch. In any case, the vote of the Grand Council of Fascism served as a pretext to remove Mussolini.

As he left the king's residence, Mussolini was put in an ambulance and taken under arrest to the Podgora Carabinieri Headquarters in the Trastevere area of Rome. In the afternoon he was transferred to the Carabinieri Cadet School in vía Legnano, where he stayed until 27 July.

Immediately after the fall of Mussolini became known, Hitler seriously considered occupying the Italian Peninsula (Operation Schwarz). Other operations he

The Campo Imperatore hotel was located next to a ski station in the Gran Sasso, Italy. (COG)

Postcard from the 1930s advertising the Campo Imperatore hotel. (COG)

considered included: the occupation of Rome and the Vatican, including the arrest of the royal family and all politicians and officers who opposed the alliance with Germany; reinstalling the fascist regime in Italy (Operation Alarico); the destruction of the Italian fleet (Operation Achse) and the liberation of Mussolini (Operation Eiche). The latter would be assigned to XI *Fliegerkorps* (XI Air Command) under the command of General Kurt Student and the objective of freeing Mussolini soon became a priority.

To accomplish the mission (code-named Operation Eiche (Operation Oak) from 1 August 1943) the first objective was to discover the whereabouts of *il Duce*, who had been missing without a trace since his last audience with the king. After staying in Rome, on 27 July he was taken to the coastal port of Gaeta, accompanied by the chief of the military police of the Supreme Command, General Francesco Saverio Pólito. Once on-board the corvette *Persefone*, he arrived on the island of Ponza at 12:00 on 28 July, where he was kept in an isolated house before spending three weeks in a private villa on the island of La Maddalena, where he had arrived on 7 August.

Initially, Student did not inform anyone about his special mission to free *il Duce*. He did not even say anything to Otto Skorzeny, the Austrian SS-Hauptsturmführer[1] whom Himmler had originally selected, together with a commando of around forty SS soldiers, for Operation Schwarz. According to Student:

> I was surprised when I received a phone call from the Führer's headquarters [*Wolfsschanze,* Wolf's Lair] while I was in Nimes on the afternoon of 26 July 1943. I was told to report to him immediately. I flew as fast as I could to Rastenburg (East Prussia), and once there was ordered by Hitler to march to Rome with all available paratroopers. I was ordered to hold Rome in case Italy surrendered and was given a special mission to free Mussolini. On the

---

1   As a general guide, the equivalent German-British Army ranks are as follows: Gefreiter (corporal); Unteroffizier (sergeant); Oberfeldwebel (sergeant major); Leutnant (second lieutenant); Oberleutnant (first lieutenant); Hauptmann (captain); Major (commander); Oberstleutnant (lieutenant colonel); Oberst (colonel). Waffen SS ranks and their corresponding British ranks are: Untersturmführer (second lieutenant); Obersturmführer (first lieutenant), Hauptsturmführer (captain); Sturmbannführer (major); Standartenführer (colonel); Obergruppenführer (general).

return trip I was accompanied by someone who was unknown to me at the time: SS-Hauptsturmführer Otto Skorzeny. We had both been given an SS commando to help search for Mussolini and carry out some police work. Hitler had ordered us to keep our instructions in the strictest silence and so we started an intense search to locate Mussolini's hiding place. Finally, on 8 September, the day that Italy surrendered, a 'hot tip' took us to the Gran Sasso. In light of this serious event, I should have put off Mussolini's rescue and committed all my forces to my main task; preventing Rome from falling into the enemy's hands.

A portrait of Major Kurt Student by Willrich. (COG)

The 'hot tip' had been given by SS-Obersturmbannführer Herbert Kappler, the commander of the German security service (SD) in Rome, who had known for several days that something strange

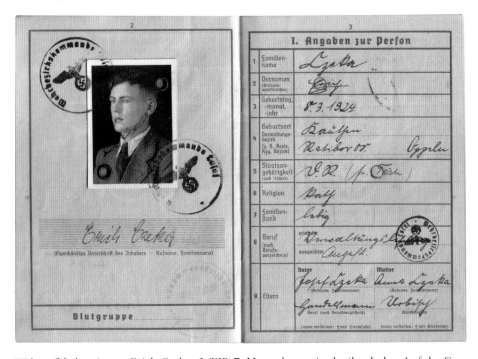

Wehrpaß belonging to Erich Czeka, 3./FJR 7. He took part in the 'land phase' of the Gran Sasso Operation, under the command of Major Mors. (COG)

The Luftwaffe eagle on a paratrooper's jump suit (CP).

was going on in the Gran Sasso. However, his suspicions were confirmed when he managed to intercept an ecrypted message addressed to the Italian police chief, Carmine Senise. Kappler knew the code used by the Italian Ministry of the Interior, so it was easy for him to decipher the message, which read, 'We have finalized the security measures in the Gran Sasso and its surroundings'. The message was signed by Inspector Gueli, and Kappler quickly communicated the information to Student, who then informed Skorzeny.

'The highest prison in the world', as it was described by Mussolini, was located in an 'unreachable and inaccessible' place in a mountain lodge called Campo Imperatore, 2,112 metres above sea level in the Italian Gran Sasso. The building itself was D-shaped and was originally planned to be the first of three buildings (the other two were never built), with the other two hotels being built in the shape of a 'V' and 'X' so that the word 'DVX' could be clearly read from above at the highest point of the Apennines. As luck would have it, the building that was erected to celebrate *il Duce* had become his prison.

Herbert Kappler, head of the German SD in Rome. This photograph was taken after he was captured by the Allies.

Student decided to free Mussolini and entrusted the task to Major Harald Mors, who was supposedly the officer most admired by Student. Mors had been part of Student's staff since the beginning of the war and in mid-July 1943 had replaced Harry Herrmann as the commander of the Fallschirmjäger-Lehr-Bataillon (the model and experimental battalion of the paratroopers), the crème de la crème, which was renamed for security reasons as I./FJR 7 (1st battalion of the 7th Regiment). As Student said: 'On the morning of 11 September, I decided to act fast and with a very particular method of attack. I could not afford to waste any more time. I entrusted the task of organising the rescue mission to the Fallschirmjäger-Lehr-Bataillon, under the command of Major Mors.' Once the alliance with the Italians was broken, there were no longer any diplomatic issues. However, there was a serious risk that Mussolini's guards, deprived of any orders due to the chaos currently reigning in the capital, (Badoglio and

Harald Mors, the paratroop commander in charge of Mussolini's rescue operation. (Illustration by Ramiro Bujeiro)

German paratrooper (Fallschirmjäger) boots. (CP)

German paratroopers in the Mediterranean, preparing for a jump. They have RZ 20 parachutes and their pale brown M38 helmets. (EC).

King Victor Manuel III having fled to Brindisi, which was now under Allied control, on the morning of 9 September), did anything terrible. From that moment, the operation to free *il Duce* was launched.

Preparing for The Mission:
Freeing Mussolini!

Harald Mors, 32, was quartered with his battalion near the Jesuit college of Mondragone. He had been talking to other officers from the battalion about the motorisation of the Fiat trucks belonging to 103rd Infantry Division *'Piacenza'* (which had been disarmed the previous day as part of the operation to control the Italian Army), when the telephone rang. At the other end was General Student, who wanted to speak to Mors about a matter of extreme urgency. After the conversation had ended, Mors set off

Luftwaffe glider pilot's badge, with C.E Juncker markings. (COG)

The glider pilots who landed at the Gran Sasso. From left to right, Gedenk, Stark, Neelmeyer, Meyer-Wehner (with cap), Berenbold, Jenniches, Heiner Lohrmann, Thielmannand and Maier. Ronsdorf is missing, as he was wounded during the landing. (COG)

Harald Mors, commander of I./FJR 7, the unit in charge of Mussolini's rescue. (COG)

for the general headquarters, where he met other officers, friends, and comrades from previous operations. He took advantage of the situation to ask the First Section commander of Student's staff, Major von Roon[2], the reason for this urgent meeting.

Ironically von Roon replied, 'Bruno Meyer', and took him to see Student. The general didn't bother with any pleasantries: 'Major, tomorrow at 07:30, free Mussolini from the Gran Sasso in Italy.' It was clear from the nature of the order what kind of pressure Student had been under over the last few days.

Student had some idea about what was entailed, but he preferred to discuss it with his right hand-man. In any case, Mors would have the freedom to act as he wished once the details of the mission were known.

> I asked for an hour to analyse the materials, the situation and my responsibilities before the mission began. It was 15:00. When I had all of the available materials in front of me, I discussed the matter with Student's intelligence officer, Hauptmann Langguth. He told me that the mission had to be carried out in the strictest secrecy. Its unofficial name, the one that was being whispered around the general staff, was 'Bruno Meyer', but more officially it was called Operation Oak (Eiche). The information that we had to hand was old and we were waiting for the arrival of a photograph of the terrain that Langguth had taken that morning.

Mors pointed out to Langguth that the information was inaccurate with many holes in it, and that there was hardly any certainty to any of it. Everything was based on vague assumptions. Langguth stated that all the information they possessed had came from Skorzeny.

> It was the first time that I had heard anything about the notorious Skorzeny [Mors declared]; a very reserved and self-assured man, who had been roaming the general headquarters for some time. No one knew what he was doing there, except that he had received a mysterious 'special mission' from Hitler

---

2   Arnold von Roon (1914-1991) was one of Student's closest associates throughout the entire war. He had been a paratrooper since 1937 and it is worth noting that he had been part of the Condor Legion during the Spanish Civil War. He made more than fifty jumps, twenty of them on the northern front and served as an observer on-board a Heinkel He 45 from A/88 squadron, which was based in Vitoria during the northern offensive. He took part in bombing raids in the Durango zone and was shot down on 27 April 1937 between Ochandiano and Ulibarri-Gamboa.

himself, and that he was an SS officer but had to wear a Luftwaffe captain's badge for security reasons.

In fact, after receiving the order to free Mussolini, Student had requested a specialist who he could trust. He niether could not nor wanted to assign this task to a paratrooper officer. Although it was a difficult mission, Skorzeny had found a way to make it work after his men had noted some special controls around the cable car station that led up to the Campo Imperatore hotel.

The information on the Gran Sasso was uncertain, but there were many indications that Mussolini was there. Student himself had taken the initiative of sending his own doctor, Dr Krutoff, to Assergi a few days before, with the excuse of looking for somewhere to house injured paratroopers. When he asked at one of the road blocks, the carabinieri responded with a curt 'no' and sent him on his way in a suspiciously abrupt way. The area was obviously under guard, but why? And more importantly, if it wasn't for Mussolini then who?

General Kurt Student, commander of the German Fallschirmjäger. (COG)

Panoramic view from the Gran Sasso, in the Abruzzo region of Italy. (EC)

After taking 60 minutes to analyse the maps and photographs for the mission, Student met with Mors again. The general explained that would be possible for paratroopers to jump out over the Assergi Valley, capture the cable car and attack the hotel. Mors voiced his concerns that the paratroopers' arrival would be seen from the hotel, thus loosing their main weapon: the element of surprise. He feared the paratroopers would alert the L'Aquilla garrison (especially the 13th and 14th Infantry Regiment and the 18th artillery regiment, '*Pinerolo*' Division. The rest of the units were in Greece).

Besides, Student's proposal seemed impossible due to the layout of the terrain itself (the hotel was near to a gorge), not to mention the strong winds and updrafts that would have scattered the paratroopers considerably, or even worse, would have smashed them against the rocks. Nor was it possible to launch a direct assault up to the hotel, which would involve climbing over 1,000 metres and putting the paratroopers within reach of the Italians. Others factors also had to be taken into account: the temperature difference between the valley bottom and 2,000 metres up the mountain, as well as the men's equipment. In an assault of this kind, the hotel garrison would have plenty of time during the long hours it would take the soldiers to climb the mountain to transfer the prisoner to a

Present view of Campo Imperatore. The astronomical observatory seen in the foreground was built after the war. (CP)

nearby cave using the various tracks and pathways available. The existing terrain near the hotel also didn't allow for any kind of transport aircraft (such as a Junkers Ju 52) to land.

All this meant that both the paratroopers' arrival and withdrawal had to be carried out by land. The most reasonable course of action would be a combined operation involving paratroopers and other soldiers driven up to the target by trucks. All troops involved would then have to return to the base using the latter vehicles.

These considerations and analysis were all taken into account with the following 'order of operations', in which Mors conceived a campaign divided in two phases; one airborne and the other by land:

Arnold von Roon, Student's assistant during the Gran Sasso operation. (CP)

- a) 1st Company (I./FJR 7), under the command of the young Oberleutnant von Berlepsch, would be part of the airborne attack and land in gliders in the vicinity of the Hotel Campo Imperatore. The company's mission (assisted by a platoon from 4th Company) would be to free *il Duce* and guard him until reinforcements arrived. Three gliders would land near the hotel and take it in a surprise attack, while the rest would be on standby with their machine guns in case of greater resistance. The nearby cable car station would also be taken so that it could be used by the reinforcements arriving from the valley over land.
- b) The bulk of the battalion, under the command of Major Harald Mors, would include two paratroop companies transported by lorries, a Panzerjäger (anti-tank) company and elements from a 'heavy weapons' company. They would be transported over land up to the Assergi Valley and occupy the town and cable car station, as well as providing the airborne troops with protection from potential attacks. It would also connect with von Berlepsch's paratroopers, if necessary, via an 'alpine' attack.
- c) After the operation was completed, all of the units would withdraw to Rome via the land route used by Major Mors. In total 380 men would be involved in the assault.

According to this plan, the airborne paratroopers' attack and thus the element of surprise were the mission's most important assets: the enemy certainly did not count on facing the possibility of such an attack. The glider pilots' training was such that they could be required to make an accurate landing, and the quick release of Mussolini would be key to preventing him from being taken by his Italian captors through the mountains. Finally, in case of a possible attack by the Italian troops based in L'Aquila, Mors proposed that he take personal command of the units arriving by trucks: 'The heavy weaponry will go with me', he concluded. In conclusion, the operation required maximum coordination between the airborne and terrestrial phases.

1. The Campo Imperatore hotel as it looks today. (CP)

2. Oberleutnant Georg von Berlepsch, commander of 1st Company that landed at Campo Imperatore. He died in Anzio, on 2 February 1944. (EC)

3. The funeral of Leutnant Heinz Weber. According to Mors, 'Nobody forgot the eleven paratroopers who fell during the fighting against the 103rd Infantry Division '*Piacenza*' three days before'. Weber fell during the fighting in Rome on 9 September 1943. His coffin is being carried on the shoulders of Italian soldiers. (B)

4. Today's view of the Campo Imperatore hotel. The cable car station is on the right of the image. (CP)

After laying out the plan to Student, Mors received the order to proceed. However, he stated that the previously-agreed timings should be delayed, as it was impossible for them to meet at the target by 07:00 the next morning. Mors requested a delay of twenty-four hours, but fears that *il Duce* would be moved yet another time meant that Student only granted a seven hour delay. Consequently, H-Hour was fixed for 14:00 on Sunday, 12 September.

Everything had been planned to perfection. Mors' analysis and subsequent proposal meant that even though the operation was creative, audacious and complicated, it was still plausible and achievable. Nothing was left to chance.

After all, the mission was to be undertaken by the elite of the German Army: the Fallschirmjäger.

All that remained was what to do with Mussolini after setting him free. Mors suggested taking him back to Rome in an armoured vehicle, which would be well-defended if placed in the centre of a column. However, Student came up with an even bolder idea: he would send his personal pilot, Hauptmann Heinrich Gerlach, to collect Mussolini aboard his Fieseler Fi-156 'Storch' (Stork), which was an extremely agile and maneuverable airplane, capable of landing on a small area such as the one in front of the hotel.

Gerlach himself describes the circumstances when he received the order:

Three days after the action at Frascati (Italy was on the verge of no longer being our ally) on 11 September 1943, I was ordered to present myself immediately before General Student. Already there was Oberst Trettner, the chief of staff of XI. Paratroop Corps, as well as Major Mors (...) Student told me about the plan to free *il Duce*. Hauptmann Skorzeny's

men had finally found their tip off: Mussolini was at the Imperatore hotel in the Gran Sasso. (...) My mission was to land a Fieseler Storch at the Campo Imperatore hotel immediately after the DFS-230 B-1 gliders. I was given the chance to offer my opinion, and, somehow, to find a solution for the task I had been entrusted with. Hauptmann Langguth showed me photographs of the Gran Sasso, along with images of the Campo Imperatore and the cable cable station that connected it to the Assergi Valley. Unfortunately the photographs had been taken from directly above and at a high altitude, meaning that it was impossible to have an accurate idea of the terrain. Langguth, who had flown over the location, could only say that the terrain was dangerously rocky with multiple obstacles. I was unable, therefore, to make sure that there was any chance of landing there with a Storch. After several minutes of intense analysis looking at the still-wet photographs, I told the general and those present: 'I will fly over and decide where the possible landing and take-offs areas can be'. The newly freed *il Duce* would then be taken to the Pratica di Mare aerodrome, where he would continue his journey on a Heinkel He 111 aircraft, accompanied by another officer.

General Student instructed me that another well-trained pilot would travel as a reserve in another Storch. If possible, I was to land next to the cable car station. Finally, Student wished me the best and told me something that I would never

3

4

forget: 'My dear Gerlach, I can't order you to land there and take off again with all the weight you will be carrying. But you should bear in mind that you can't crash with Mussolini on board following his liberation.' (...) I called Staffel C and ordered two Storchs be prepared for a special operation the following morning. OFw. Hundt was to be the pilot of the second plane, and he would be notified of the route to follow the next morning.

The conversation between Mors and Student continued, the latter pointing out to Mors that Hitler was very interested in the success of the mission and wanted to see his friend Mussolini freed. If the operation failed then the paratroopers would lose their prestige. Mussolini had to be taken to Rome, dead or alive.

It is important to highlight the fact that at this moment in time, Skorzeny's involvement in the mission had not been planned, nor was he present at the meeting between Student and Mors. A few days earlier, on the morning of 8 September, he had met Student in Frascati after having made the reconnaissance flight with Langguth over the Gran Sasso. Student had told him

1. German paratroopers in Rome on 9 September 1943. The 75 mm LG40 was a common gun among the paratroopers. (B).

2. The most characteristic garment worn by the German paratrooper was the jump smock, known as *knochensack* (bone bag). The model seen in this image is wearing the chipped camouflage pattern, which was used during Mussolini's rescue. (MDMC)

3. German paratrooper M 38 helmet. (CP)

4. Representation of a German paratrooper during the Gran Sasso raid. In this operation, as in the previous days in Rome, the FG 42 sub-machine gun was used, which had been specifically designed for the paratroopers.(Illustration by Ramiro Bujeiro)

The inside of a German DFS-230 aeroplane showing paratroopers sitting in a central row. As well as the lack of space, another difficulty was that half of the crew had to travel facing backwards. (COG)

'Dear Captain, thank you for everything you have done. Your contribution to the search has been very important, but now your mission is over. The execution of the rescue operation will be carried out by my paratroopers.' Skorzeny had played no role in the planning of the mission.

Skorzeny Joins the Operation

After speaking with Student, Mors was authorised to call the battalion to declare the state of emergency, and to inform the company commanders of what they needed to know for the mission, without actually telling them what the objective was.

Later, Student telephoned Mondragone and warned Mors of a slight change of plan: the Austrian officer Otto Skorzeny would be taking part in the mission and would present himself immediately. Mors did not object to his joining mission (he had no reason to at the time), but it did mean that he had to sacrifice sixteen paratroopers in order to free up space for the same number of SS soldiers. Skorzeny had clearly not resigned himself to the idea of staying out of the operation, and had asked Student if he could participate, along with some of his men.

Mors told Student that there was a 'formal' problem concerning military hierarchy. As a captain, Skorzeny couldn't be under the command of Oberleutnant von Berlepsch (a lieutenant), who was in charge of landing near the hotel with 1st Company. Student solved the problem (by phone, as always) by assuring Major Mors that Skorzeny would be subordinated to him: 'He will have no authority and is participating purely as an observer, one could say even as a political adviser.' Soon afterwards, Skorzeny appeared before Mors, who until that moment had never

Otto Skorzeny was awarded the Knight's Cross of the Iron Cross following the Gran Sasso raid and was celebrated as a hero at an event held at the Sport Palace, Berlín, on 3 October 1943. (B)

1 exchanged words with the paratroop commander. Meanwhile, Mors himself was distrustful of the Austrian.

Skorzeny had got what he wanted: to be involved in the operation with his men. This was no doubt granted as a reward and in recognition of the work he had carried out during the hunt for *il Duce*'s whereabouts.

However, Skorzeny was not to hold any command in the rescue.

Richard Kloes was a member of 4th Company (4./FJR 7), and although he did not participate in the Gran Sasso operation, he clearly remembers what Skorzeny and his men were doing as they were encamped with the paratroopers:

4th Company, to which I belonged, was ordered to occupy a maritime radio station located in Ariccia, near Rome. The Italian resistance broke quickly thanks to the fact that we attacked with light artillery (Leichtgeschütz 42-2, 105 mm calibre). There were casualties on both sides, but once the Italian soldiers were finally disarmed, they went home.

I was the first machine gunner and had to protect one of the main guns. As well as disarming this little garrison, I also took part in another action that same day: 'disarming' a military hospital. Clearly, no doctor or nurse thought about resisting, and our task was to requisition some of the doctors' pistols.

As we were returning to the camp at Frascati, airplanes towing the gliders for the Gran Sasso raid flew over our heads as we passed through Pratica di Mare.

1. Luftwaffe belt buckle. The shape of the eagle's tale indicates that was one of the first models to be manufactured. (CP)

2. Sergeant Eugen Abel together with his men during the fighting in Rome on 9 September. These paratroopers would later participate in the Gran Sasso raid. Abel survived the war and lived in the German Democratic Republic. (CP)

3. Detail of the German paratrooper jump smock. (CP)

The battalion camp alternated between a field of olive trees at Frascati and a chestnut grove near the Alban Hills, next to Lake Albano, in Ariccia. It was while the battalion was encamped at the latter place [days before the operation], when twelve to fifteen soldiers appeared dressed in Luftwaffe uniforms, put up their tents and were fed by my company. They used Wehrmacht vehicles, as well as civilian ones with Italian registration numbers, used infantry

weapons from time to time, and were frequently absent during the whole day. However, they were never identified as Waffen-SS members. It was clear to us that they had a special mission, especially because of the type of vehicles and equipment they were using (e.g. radios). Their continued absences, as well as the activities they carried out, which had no connection with ours, provided further evidence of the special nature of their mission. After learning of Mussolini's liberation, it was clear to us that the officer in charge of the group had not been a Luftwaffe captain, but an SS officer called Otto Skorzeny.

Everyone wore the Luftwaffe tropical uniform for camouflage and to help hide their presence. They lived with the paratroop battalion encamped on the shores of Lake Albano, before moving to the outskirts of Frascati,

4. Richard Kloes, a Fallschirmjäger in 4./FJR. As other units of the second paratroop division, the 1./FJR 7 took part in the action disarming the Italian troops on 9 September. Its objectives were the 103th Infantry Division '*Piacenza*' the 111th Infantry Regiment and the 37th Artillery Regiment. The Fallschirmjäger were deployed in Albano, Ariccia and Genzano, locations near the Albano mountains. Some sections of 4th Company didn't participate in the Gran Sasso raid, because they remained in Rome. Kloes' section was one of them. (COG)

1. Cloth cartridge cases for the German Kar 98 rifle. Another of the paratrooper's typical item of clothing. (MB44)

2. A 'gravity' penknife that all paratroopers and Luftwaffe personnel carried (MB44).

3. Plaque commemorating Mussolini's stay at the Campo Imperatore hotel. 'Benito Mussolini was held prisoner in this hotel from 28 August to 12 September 1943.'

rather than at General Student's headquarters. Skorzeny's men also assisted the paratroopers in disarming the Italian '*Piacenza*' Division, south of Frascati on 7 and 8 September.

To return to the story, Student had made one final mistake, which was allowing Skorzeny to be involved in the operation. He must have thought that he could trust him with the transfer of *il Duce*, once he had been freed. He certainly had good reasons for believing so: the captain had been ordered to return to Germany once the mission had been completed; he had been in the Wolf's Lair several times and knew Hitler personally; he was from Vienna, which might be useful if the plane stopped there on its way to the Führer's headquarters. All of this meant that the Austrian was the ideal man to have on board and to be *il Duce*'s personal escort. Mors and Student completely agreed on this last aspect, and were happy to avoid handing such an uncomfortable task over to a paratroop officer. In the current situation in Italy, officers were irreplaceable - a simple, practical consideration that would have been enough to completely alter the events that led to the liberation of Mussolini. However, the two men were still far from suspecting this.

4

First Company Heads for the Gran Sasso

Bernard Bosshammer was a Spieß (sergeant major) in 1st Company. The company was commanded by Baron Georg von Berlepsch, who had been in combat in the deserts of Tunisia under the command of General Ramcke. Bosshammer, who was charged with the most difficult part of the operation: landing near the hotel, spoke in detail of how the events unfurled:

> We were quartered in the 'Collegio Nobile Mondragone' [Jesuit school] in Frascati. Throughout the whole the day of the 11th we were testing the weapons, equipment and vehicles that had been confiscated from the Italians so that we could use them in the near future. I was in a communications truck that had been seized in Albano. We were busy writing reports on the action 1st Company had been involved in against the Italian Army, as well as writing up casualty lists.

A DF-230 glider being towed through the skies over Italy. (COG)

Bernd Bosshammer, sergeant major in 1st Company and a veteran of jumps in Rotterdam and Crete, was one of the paratroopers that landed in Campo Imperatore (COG).

Oberleutnant Georg Freiherr von Berlepsch was in another store 40 metres away from my truck. Our phone rang incessantly. A telephone call informed us that a battalion transmission unit was going to be added to the company, under the command of Fw. Herbert Ripke, as well as a radio unit and two more health units. All of this meant that action was expected. In the afternoon, von Berlepsch went to General Headquarters in Frascati and returned at 22:00 with some documents and photographs. Next, all the section chiefs were called to his tent, where we were instructed on the importance and the secrecy of the operation. This was confirmation that we were heading for action. Instead of using parachutes we would use DFS-230 B-1 gliders (together with some C-1s, with braking rockets in the nose), which we had been trained with near Laval, France.

We were shown the target and objectives of each action and kept them secret. We were not informed of the exact place where we were going to carry out the mission, nor were we given any names. The photographs were confusing and only showed a large area of ground on a mountainside. The only thing that was said was that an important person was being guarded there by around 200 soldiers. There was even talk of elite troops. The areas where the gliders were to land were marked with a cross. Each section was given its instructions and the orders were then passed on to each platoon (ie, the occupants of a glider: nine soldiers and the pilot). Inner plans of the building to be attacked were also handed out, a task entrusted to Fahnenjunker Fw. Eugen Abel, who had been a Latin teacher before the war at a school in Saarland. He spoke perfect French and fairly acceptable Italian, and spent an hour with von Berlepsch preparing his 'role' in the operation.

At 06:15 on 12 September 1943, the section chiefs informed the troops about the details of the operation. After checking the weapons, ammunition and equipment one last time, the company commander gave the order to climb into the trucks. The column set off at 07:00 and reached the Pratica di Mare aerodrome, near Rome, around 09:00. There, on the runway, we saw Skorzeny for the very first time, along with his men wearing the tropical uniform of the Luftwaffe. They were not wearing traditional paratrooper helmets, but rather the regular Wehrmacht ones. They were also not wearing jump suits, so they were easily recognisable.

About 10:00, we understood that General Student had arrived. He talked with the officers and glider pilots, and we later learned that we were going to the Gran Sasso to free *il Duce*. The operation should be carried out without

Paratroopers from 1./FJR 7 getting ready to board one of the gliders and set off from Pratica di Mare to the Gran Sasso (S).

too much resistance and we were given express orders not to shoot, unless the Italians did so first.

It was then that we realized Skorzeny[3] and his men would be flying with us, which meant that one of our paratrooper groups would have to stay behind.

To our surprise, we were worried to see that there were only ten gliders, instead of the planned twelve, which meant that some of our comrades would have to stay behind.

3   Harald Mors and Bernhard Bosshammer took part in the operation's 50th anniversary celebrations. A room in the cable car station down the valley was used to greet the guests, among whom were the historians Arrigo Petacco, Marco Patricelli, Antonio Spinosa, Giuseppe Tricoli, Giordano Bruno Guerri and Sergio Zavoli. After a few words from Mors, who was listened to with silence and concentration, the journalists asked the two veterans if Skorzeny had been in command of the operation. Bosshammer answered, 'We hadn't met Skorzeny before; he didn't give us any orders (…) The orders were given before the operation. Each Oberjäger and Feldwebel knew what their men had to do. No other orders were given to us about the Gran Sasso raid. The orders for 1st Company were given by Oberleutnant Freiherr von Berlepsch.' Mors commented that, 'The complex political operation, which began with a direction from the State and ended with the liberation mission carried out by us, was beyond our responsibility. My words came from a military officer's point of view. Politics did not belong in our mission.'

It was very hard for our commander to decide who should miss out, because everything had been planned around the full team of paratroopers. Those who had to stay behind were disappointed and upset because the mission was about freeing *il Duce* and they wanted to be present when it happened.

About 12:00, the aerial alarm was sounded and the Flak batteries opened fire. Everybody ran to find cover as a formation of bombers flew over the airfield. After a while we heard their bombs. We had been very lucky.

And if all this wasn't enough, Skorzeny had prepared a surprise that didn't appear in the rescue plan. Bosshammer continues:

Suddenly we saw that the Lufwaffe soldiers were accompanied by an Italian general. We learned later that it was the police general, Fernando Soleti, who had been held in Rome. General Student explained to him that he was to accompany the group so that the Italian soldiers would not open fire. His presence would hopefully avoid any an unnecessary bloodshed. Soleti was pale. He looked like he wanted to shoot himself with his gun.

The decision to bring along Fernando Soleti was made entirely by Skorzeny. Unlike Student, he was convinced that Mussolini's captors would fight back, and this worried him. He thought that the gliders would be an easy target for the 20 mm machine guns which, according to his information, had been set up around the hotel. He was also afraid that the hardness of the terrain would make landing difficult, and if any problems were encountered and the gliders were scattered over

More paratroopers at Pratica di Mare. On the right is Gerhard Opel, platoon leader in 4th Company, who died in 2005. (S)

the area, then the paratroopers would be an easy target for the '200 rifles' that guarded the building. Skorzeny's assistant, Obersturmführer Karl Radl, said that, 'to ward off any danger, we had no option but to take a high-ranking Italian officer on board. We were convinced that his presence would rattle the Italians.'

Soleti was a brigadier general in the PAI [*Polizia dell'Africa italiana*], rather than a general in the carabinieri, as he is often mistakenly referred to. His presence was intended to prevent the guards from killing Mussolini, following the orders of his superiors and thus preventing his release. According to Skorzeny, Soleti 'had shown favour towards the Germans'. This may have been true, but it is more likely that he had no intention of embarking on the adventure of Mussolini's liberation. General Soleti had to explain to *il Duce* himself about his ambiguous presence, just before they were taking off from the Gran Sasso. Soleti had actually performed an important role in the events surrounding Mussolini arrest in July 1943 and his presence had been requested by Obersturmbannführer SS Herbert Kappler, the head of the SD Security Service in Rome. Student tolerated his being there, no doubt bending under Skorzeny's insistence. Mors wrote:

While camped at Assergi following the liberation of *il Duce*, I could tell from von Berlepsch that Skorzeny and his assistant Radl had taken an Italian general called Soleti to the airfield that morning. According to Skorzeny, Student had requested the Italian's participation to avoid bloodshed. If the soldiers on duty saw an Italian general in uniform get off a glider and order them not to shoot, then they would quickly hand over their weapons. I don't know if Student knew that Soleti had been forcibly taken from home and driven to the airfield. Nor if Student knew that Soleti had tried to commit suicide with his pistol before boarding the glider, which is why he had been disarmed by

Otto Skorzeny at Campo Imperatore. Unlike the paratroopers, he and his men wore Luftwaffe combat trousers and jackets, with no jump smocks, and carried a standard M 42 helmet. (Illustration by Ramiro Bujeiro)

(*Above*) Cable car station at Campo Imperatore. The cabin seen in the photograph is the one that was operating in September 1943.

(*Below*) Mussolini's room (201) at the Campo Imperatore hotel.

'Skorzeny's guest'. The frightened General Soleti (right), next to the glider flown by Oberfeldwebel Berenbold (EC).

the SS soldiers. However, I knew Student's education as a Prussian officer and I can't imagine that his ethics as an officer would consciously approve of this flagrant outrage contrary to the Hague Convention and to traditional German military values. Berslepsch was more than upset as this meant that he had to leave another man from his company on the ground. According to him, once they reached the Gran Sasso, the Italian gesticulated wildly and merely increased the confusion, without actually playing any role in the liberation. Not that this mattered anyway, as there had been no form of resistance from the Italians.

5

An Unexpected Manoeuvre

The operation was to begin at 13:00. Bernd Bosshammer recalls, 'We got on the gliders, which would be drawn by Henschel Hs 126 aircraft. Ten machines with nine soldiers and a pilot in each amounted to a total of 100 soldiers. Also travelling in the group were two war correspondents: Leutnant Bruno von Kayser (sent by the *Illustrierte Beobachter* newspaper), and Oberjäger Toni Schneiders.' The unit in charge of transportation was 12./LLG1, based in Valence, France.

Skorzeny's men occupied two gliders. Skorzeny travelled in the fourth with General Soleti and some of his men, among whom was Leutnant Warger (his translator) and Untersturmführer Otto Schwerdt. Obersturmführer Karl Radl and the rest of the SS were in the fifth glider in the formation. Skorzeny's pilot was the experienced Leutnant Elimar Meyer-Wehner. He had not originally been assigned to the Austrian's aircraft, but as he explains himself, 'I noticed that Skorzeny and the Italian were set to fly with a young pilot with no experience in this type of action. I already knew from Crete the difference between training flights and the real thing, which is why I decided to take the controls of this important glider.'

The airborne operation is underway as the Hs-126 planes tow the DFS-230 to the release point. (EC)

Bruno von Kayser photographed the Campo Imperatore from glider No. 6, moments before landing. Skorzeny's glider had already landed next to the hotel. (EC)

They took off on time. The gliders flew in groups (*Kette*) of three aircraft. Travelling in the first Hs-126 was Hauptmann Langguth, the General Staff's intelligence officer, who knew the terrain following several reconnaissance flights. In the first formation was von Berlepsch's glider (at the head of the formation). The second group contained the glider flown by Leutnant Meyer-Wehner, while the rest of the company flew in the final *Kette*. The tenth glider flew behind the groups as a separate aircraft and contained Bosshammer.

The gliders flew over Tivoli towards Campo Imperatore. The flight passed without major incident, but something did occur that altered the order of the formation, and it is important to discuss what happened as it did effect the development of events.

The first group carried out a manoeuvre to gain height, but the second group did not follow and consequently, Skorzeny's glider now found itself at the head of the formation. The reason why the first group acted this way has never been made clear. According to Bosshammer, Skorzeny must have spoken with the Hs 126 pilot towing his glider (Obtl. Johannes Heidenreich) before take off, meaning the manoeuvre had already

Hs 126 Crews	
Pilot	Observer
Ofw. Heilig	Oblt. Johannes Heidernreich
Uffz. Hartmann	Gefr. Otto
Fw. Anders	Ogfr. Zielinsky
Fw. Hommers	Ogfr. Stäblein
Fw. Gerhard	Gfr. Torka
Ofw. Geuel	Haptm. Langguth
Fw. Wengenmeier	Ogfr. Stepper
Ofw. Walters	Ogfr. Seifert
Fw. Hornschurhb	Ogfr. Kruger

been planned so that Skorzeny and his men were the first ones to land at the Gran Sasso. This explanation is also confirmed by Hans Joachim Kurth. According to him, 'Even Heidenreich himself confessed after the war that Skorzeny and he had secretly agreed to put the Austrian at the head of the formation at all costs, so that he would be the first one to land.'

A rough version of what occurred is given by Elimar Meyer-Wehner, who was indirectly involved. He states that,

> I remained in my assigned position, climbing with difficulty due to the strong winds. However, once I gained altitude, the situation was much calmer so I was able to focus my attention on other things. I looked around and saw that the other planes were flying without any issues and that the one behind was approaching little by little. At the same time I could also see the great beauty of the terrain that we were flying over. I tried to comment on this with the translator behind me (General Soleti was sitting behind him, with Skorzeny next),[4] but I suddenly realised that the aircraft at the head of the formation had banked right in a wide arc, almost as if he was trying to return to Rome. The second and third gliders followed his course. What was going on? In the plane towing me, 30 metres away, I saw the head of Henschel's squad, Oberletnant Heidenreich at the observer's post. He had left his position at the head of Langguth's formation, who knew the way very well thanks to his reconnaissance flights. Heidenreich checked the time. There was no time left if we wanted to be over the target by 14:00! The actions of the lead group

---

4   Kurth points out, 'This explanation is necessary in order to make clear that, during the flight, Skorzeny was unable to give orders. Apart from the fact that it was none of his concern, no pilot would have tolerated any such intervention.'

1. The Dashboard of a DFS-230 glider. (COG)

2. Hitching up the tow-plane and the DFS-230. (COG)

seemed incomprehensible to us. After giving me a knowing look, he ordered his pilot to continue flying straight to the target. Thanks to this decision we returned to Student's plan, although my glider was now at the head of the formation.'

Gerhard Langguth, the protagonist of the manoeuvre, tried to explain what happened after the war:

The manoeuvre carried out during the approach was not planned. As I was responsible for the aircraft, I gave the orders. I decided to do this because, according to my assessment, after takeoff it was not certain that all of the gliders would be able to reach sufficient altitude in order to clear the high ground

Waffen SS Poster with the heading 'Auch Du' (You too). (CP)

near Tivoli. This had proved to be a problem when I flew the Heinkel 111 on 8 September, during one of my reconnaissance flights. On the other hand, the formation was two or three minutes ahead of schedule, but as there was no radio link with the rest of the gliders, the manoeuvre was not understood by the other aircraft and so the formation had to be modified. Despite this, the group landed at the target on schedule. Thanks to the fact that a pilot had misunderstood the manoeuvre, Skorzeny was now heading the formation. I understand that General Student disapproved of my initiative, which might

The FG 42 (Fallschirmjägergewehr 42) sub-machine gun, specifically designed for paratroopers, was a revolutionary weapon that was used for the very first time in 1943. (CP).

1. Glider pilot Uffz. Gustav Thielmann was awarded the German Gold Cross following the Gran Sasso raid. He also took part in the operation on Osel Island (14/09/1941) and in Operation Rösselsprung (the mission to capture Tito in Yugoslavia). His awards include: Iron Cross 2nd Class, Iron Cross 1st Class, German Cross in Gold (cloth), Glider Pilot Badge (in cloth), Civilian Glider Pilot Badge and the Croatian Insignia of Valour.

2. Leutnant Elimar Meyer-Wehner, a member of 12./LLG 1, wearing the Knight's Cross he was awardedfollowing his actions at the Gran Sasso. He flew glider n°4, the aircraft Skorzeny was travelling in. (SD)

have affected the operation, but politically it gave Skorzeny the possibility of being responsible for anything that went wrong in a role that didn't belong to him, as all the elements of the operation were in Student's hands anyway.

This manoeuvre that favoured Skorzeny occurred around 100 kilometres from the Gran Sasso, before we reached Tivoli, and not near the Gran Sasso, as he states.

And so it was this strange and unplanned action, along with the consequent misunderstanding between the pilots, that would turn Skorzeny into the group's leader.

His subsequent decision of a diving landing, contrary to the orders given by Student, would cause great tension among the officers. Mors noticed such a tension when arriving at the hotel, even before they reached Mussolini:

Waffen SS propaganda poster. (CP)

When we reached the hotel reception, Berlepsch and the war correspondent von Kayser informed me (...) the group of airplanes with their respective gliders had taken off well and without any problems. In any case, there was a mistake regarding the planned flight formation. The aircrafts had no communication system between them and both the formation and group order was altered. However, this did should not have had any consequences in terms of discipline and carrying out our orders.

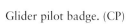

The towing planes cast off the gliders at a height of 2,300 metres and a distance of 4 kilometres from the target. After an initial pass, the DFS 230 went behind the spur of the mountain to fool the Italians into

Glider pilot badge. (CP)

thinking that their target was not Campo Imperatore. According to Bosshammer, 'Through a small window of the glider I could see trucks and a great trail of dust. These must have surely been our vehicles with the other battalion companies. Soon afterwards we saw the hotel and seconds later we landed around 100-150 metres from it.'

Heiner Lohrmann, glider pilot. Curiously, he is seen here wearing the motor pilot badge. The glider pilot badge was introduced on 16 December 1940. According to the regulations, two Luftwaffe pilot badges could not be worn at the same time, (In Lohrmann's case, he was both a qualified glider and motorised aircraft pilot). The choice of which badge to wear depended on the unit to which the pilot was assigned. (JH)

6

The 'Ground Phase'

The 'ground phase' of the operation began at 03:00 on 12 September. The motorised column heading towards the Gran Sasso was composed of the General Staff and the battalion's 2nd and 3rd companies. Among other machines, the group included two armoured vehicles, mainly in case Mussolini had to be transferred by land.

As soon as the journey began, a German armoured vehicle appeared on the road, obliging Mors' column to take a diversion. In addition, fighting was known to have taken place between the *Regio Esercito* and the *Wermacht*, not to mention the civilian population, who themselves had started harassing German troops. Mors did not want to take the risk of his men entering into any combat at the beginning of their journey, which is why he took a detour. This meant

1. Paratroopers from Mors' ground column. (EQ)

2. German paratroopers badge, stamped by the Dresden jeweler, G.H Osang. (COG)

3. Eric Czeka from 3rd Company. He qualified as a paratrooper twenty days before the Gran Sasso raid took place. In February 1944 he was awarded the Iron Cross 2nd Class. (COG)

4. The cable car from Assergi to Campo Imperatore. (EC)

that the planned 240 kilometre journey they should have taken, was now 60 kilometres longer. Added to the difficulties of negotiating enemy territory was the problem of driving the trucks themselves. The Fiat trucks had been confiscated in the operation against the *'Piacenza'* division and the drivers were unused to having the steering wheel on the right-hand side. Only the vehicles in the armoured company were manufactured in Germany. 'The typical late summer night was splendid', Mors recalled. 'You could count the stars in the sky.' As dawn broke, the temperature, heat, dust and thirst would increase.

The column reached L'Aquila without any mishaps at 13:00. Telephone lines were cut in order to isolate the Campo Imperatore hotel. At 13:45, Mors looked at the hotel through his binoculars and before entering the Assergi Valley, ordered a detachment led by Leutnant Weber to occupy the cable car station.

Earlier, after flying over Assergi (around 18 kilometres), the paratroopers had opened fire against a forest guard, Pasqualino Di Tocco, who

was trying to block the road at a control point. Di Tocco was wounded and would die the following day in the civilian hospital at L'Aquila. Weber's men occupied the cable car station, killing a carabinieri, Giovanni Natali, in the process. These two men would be the only victims of the operation.

Soon after, the DFS-230 gliders appeared. The coordination throughout the operation had been perfect. Mors still had a further 200 metres to go in order to reach the cable car station, which was already occupied by Weber and his men, when the driver of the truck carrying the radio signaled to approach. With great joy, the radio operator, Liutenant Karl Heinz Blumenthal, gave him a sheet of paper on which was written a single, eloquent phrase: '*Aufgrag erfüllt!*' (Mission accomplished!). It was 14:17. Mors couldn't believe that the operation had been completed so quickly and so perfectly. The question still remained whether or not Mussolini was dead or alive. After asking, the answer he received left him in no doubt: 'Alive!'

1. Two radio operators in one of Mors' trucks. On the left is Leutnant Karl-Heinz Blumenthal. (B)

2. Karl Ziegler was born in 1924 and was member of 3rd Company. After the Gran Sasso raid he fought in Anzio/Nettuno, where he was seriously wounded, and in the outskirts of Paris. He was captured in Bastogne at the end of 1994. (COG)

3. Hermann Wollter was a veteran of the Grann Sasso raid, where he was the head of 3rd Platoon, 2nd Company. (COG)

4. Two members of Mors' column are seen covered in dust after many hours of travelling. (B)

7

Landing at 'Campo Imperatore'

What had happened on the mountain? A quick outcome where only a single shot had been fired, thus fulfilling the mission in the best way possible – in under fifteen minutes. Bosshammer continues his detailed account of how the events unfolded:

> There was a strong pull on my glider when it touched down. The landing skates were covered with barbed wire and the braking parachute was also deployed. I hit my left knee on the edge of the glider and suddenly felt a strong pain. I also noticed that there was considerable bleeding from the wound. Every step I took was painful, but I had to continue with the mission. Our group's objective was to secure the rear exit. All of the Italian soldiers guarding *il Duce* were visibly surprised [to see us], but no one

Waffen SS skull. (MB 44)

The glider flown by Leutnant
Meyer-Wehner, parked next to the hotel. (EC)

made any efforts to stop us. A shot rang out as we climbed out of the glider. Oberjäger Willi Irrgang (this was his first action), hadn't secured his rifle and so it had fired into the air. However, due to our nervousness during these first moments, few of us realised this at the time. Another glider had landed in the same place as us and had also had an improvised and jerky landing. Oberleutnant von Berlepsch had landed around 150 metres from us. Panting, he climbed to the top where the hotel was, and then around to the main entrance. Eugen Abel, who had landed by the main entrance, was already there. The Italian soldiers were watching what we were doing, and had no idea who we were; English, American or German. Meanwhile, General Soleti stood in front of the hotel and ordered the soldiers not to shoot. Mussolini was peering out of a window from the second floor of the hotel. Ten minutes later he left the hotel and remained in the main hall for a few minutes, surrounded by German and Italian soldiers. Skorzeny was behind him. I limped over to where they were stood, but stayed around twenty paces away. The Italian soldiers had to leave their weapons in the large dining-room at the entrance of the hotel, but the officers were allowed to keep their pistols.

1. To prepare for the mission, Mors and Student only had a few photographs of the terrain. This image shows the initial landing plan and the one that was actually executed (gliders in circles). (COG, via Hans Joachim Kurth)

2. German paratrooper's gloves. (CP)

3. The glider, piloted with great skill by Meyer-Wehner, landed only a few metres away from the target. Skorzeny was traveling in this aircraft. (COG)

4 & 5. After Mussolini's release, war reporters Toni Schneiders and Bruno von Kayser photographsed the paratroopers simulating the attack. In one of the photographs, an Italian soldier watches on. (EC)

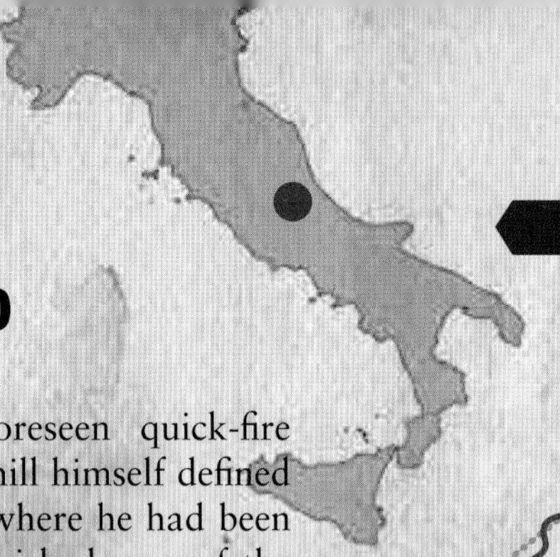

8

Gran Sasso

On 12 September 1943, an unforeseen quick-fire paratrooper operation, which Churchill himself defined as audacious, freed Mussolini from where he had been hidden by Badoglio. Before the astonished gaze of the Italian garrison, 100 Fallschirmjäger landed in gliders near the Campo Imperatore hotel.

FIESELER FI-156 STORCH

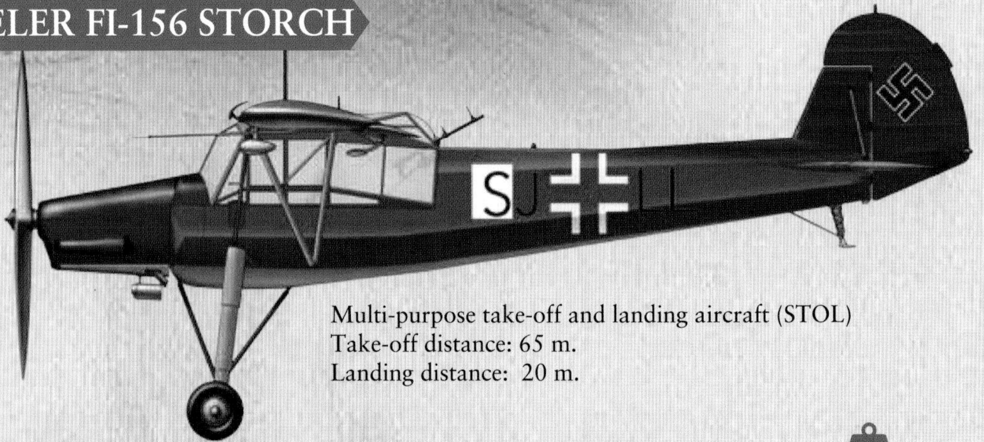

Multi-purpose take-off and landing aircraft (STOL)
Take-off distance: 65 m.
Landing distance: 20 m.

MAXIMUM SPEED
175 Km/h

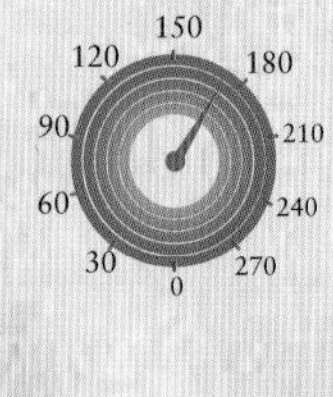

WEAPONS
1 7,92 mm MG 15 machine gun
Length: 9,9 m 
Size: 14,3 m

FLIGHT AUTONOMY
2 hours

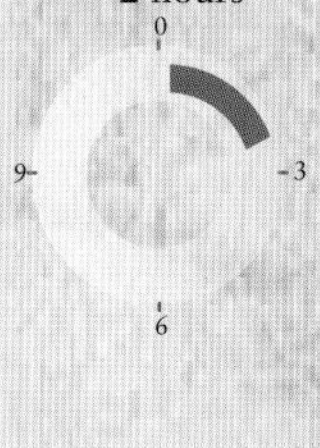

MAXIMUM HEIGHT 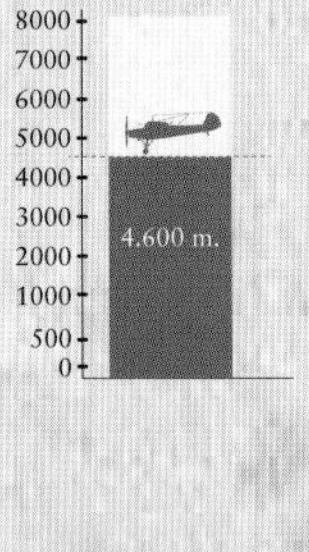 
4.600 m.

KG
Unladen weight
930 Kg

Crew:
1 pilot + 1 soldier

GLIDER DFS230

MAXIMUM SPEED

161 Km/h

Length: 11,3 m
Size: 21,1 m

MAXIMUM HEIGHT

8000
7000
6000
5000
4000
3000
2000 4.600 m.
1000
500
0

Crew
1 pilot + 9 soldiers

KG
Unladen weight:
770 kg.
Load:
1.240 kg

Glider DFS 230
Production : 1.600 units

CAMPO IMPERATORE

Glider and Fi-156 distribution around the hotel

N E S

LEGEND

Direction of take off by Gerlach's Fieseler «Storch»

A Glider 1 (von Berlepsch)
B Glider 2
C Glider 3
D Glider 4 (Skorzeny)
E Glider 5 (Mendel/Radl)
F Glider 6 (Von Kayser/ Toni Schneiders – war correspondent)
G Glider 7 (Abel)
H Glider 8
I Glider 9 (Opel)
J Glider 10 (Bosshammer; machine guns and sanitaries)

CABLE CAR STATION

HOTEL

Leutnant Gerard Opel was the commander of 2nd Platoon, 4./FJR 7. This was the only group from 4th Company which took part, as the 1st and 3rd companies were occupying Rome. Opel remembers the release of *il Duce*:

> The officers and a large number of the soldiers who were guarding Mussolini were napping. Only a few carabinieri were near the hotel when we landed. Once we arrived, my mission was to occupy the cable car station so that the troops down in Assergi could ascend to where we were. I remember how a trembling Italian soldier approached me and handed me his weapon. He pointed down to where three of his comrades had hidden, their weapons abandoned in a corner. I later learned that they belonged to a unit that had fought valiantly with our troops on the Eastern Front.

Nicolás Hoelscher was in the same company as Bosshammer: According to him:

1. A piece of the glider, piloted by Ronsdorf, which was found at Campo Imperatore in 2010. (MD)

2. Gerhard Opel in France, 1944. His is wearing a shirt with the Italian camouflage style, a characteristic seen in certain German clothing from 1943 to 1945 when using material requisitioned from the Italian army. (COG)

3. General Fernando Soleti talks to one of the glider pilots, Oberfeldwebel Berenbold. The man in black is Mussolini's personal secretary. (EC)

As a corporal in the battalion I was 18 years old when I took part in the attack on the Gran Sasso. We found around eighty soldiers in the hotel, and another forty in the cable car station. We didn't come across any resistance, perhaps due to the surprise arrival of our gliders, as well as the fact that most of the soldiers were either eating or sleeping. I didn't hear a single shot and my comrades who attacked the station told me the same. The hotel was occupied quickly without the slightest resistance and our mission was reduced to disarming the carabinieri, who looked surprised when after taking their weapons, we told them to go home. And so the Italian guard surrendered without any complications, which was better for everyone. Some of the aeroplanes that had towed us there were still flying over our heads trying to protect us. Mussolini's voice could clearly be heard shouting from his window, 'What are you doing? Do you not see that he is an Italian general! Don't shoot! Everything is in order.' He was clearly referring to Soleti.

9

Mors Meets Mussolini

After this critical moment, Mors headed up to the hotel in the cable car. He was accompanied by his assistant, Leutnant Hans Joachim Kurth, Feldwebel Wächtler (his interpreter), Oberleutnant Karl Schulze, 3rd Company commander, and some of his paratroopers. Before coming up, Mors had already spoken to von Berlepsch and a very succinct conversation had taken place between them:

  - Losses?
  - None, Herr Major.
  - And il Duce?
  - He's preparing his luggage.

Mors' group would reach the hotel at 14.45 The wind at the summit was strong and persistent.

Mors and von Berlepsch meeting at Campo Imperatore. From left to right; Alois Hermann, Karl Sculze (whose autograph can be seen on the photograph), Mors and von Berlepsch. The scene is being filmed by Schneiders. (COG)

Baron von Berlepsch was the first to meet Mors and informed him of the situation. He was calm. At that moment, the engine of Gerlach's plane was heard as it came in to land. Everybody was smiling: the German soldiers because of their successful mission, the Italians because perhaps, with the liberation of *il Duce*, the strain from holding such an important prisoner in custody would now be lifted. The guards mingled with their former German comrades as they surrendered their weapons. Mors looked around and noticed that all the gliders were scattered around the hotel. All except for one, which was around 300 metres away on a rough, steep ramp, and had been partially damaged (red flares were being fired from it as a distress signal). He could see that the medical officer, Dr Brunner, was assisting the wounded.

Mors thought that the cause of the accident had happened during the flight, although he didn't rule out that the glider could have attempted a crash-landing manoeuvre, instead of gliding, as General Student had expressly ordered. According to Student, the gliders had to land in strict order and as simultaneously as possible, so that the Italians would not be able to target isolated groups of paratroopers. To that effect, a landing plan was established.

(*Left*) Skulls of the Waffen SS in BeVo fabric. (CP)

(*Right*) Oberjäger Klaus Jacobi uses a Torn. Fu. D2 VHF/AM radio to inform Student's Headquarters that the operation has been successful. Jacobi was reported MIA on 1 February 1944, in Ponto Rotto, near Cisterna. (EC)

However, Skorzeny had disobeyed this order, telling his pilot, Meyer-Wehner, to carry out a 'dive' landing. In this first meeting with Berlepsch and the war correspondent Bruno von Kayser, Mors noticed the tension and coldness between the 'arrogant and overconfident' Skorzeny and the rest of the paratroopers.

> You could see that Skorzeny tried to stay by Mussolini and didn't want to lose contact with him under any circumstances. I sensed a cold tension on the faces of Berlepsch and von Kayser, and guessed that something had happened, and the hostile tension was a direct consequence of this.

He couldn't fully get into the matter because *il Duce* arrived, followed by his secretary. Mors described the encounter:

> I introduced myself as the major in charge of the mission. I told him that he would be taken to the Führer's headquarters in Germany. Mussolini shook my hand and thanked me, very politely, in German. He repeated what he had said to Berlepsch shortly before, 'I was sure that my friend Hitler would not let me down'. You could see the signs of disappointment and suffering

1. Captain Gerlach's Fi-156 'Storch' after it had landed on Campo Imperatore (EC).

2. Waffen SS belt buckle. Next to the Eagle is the inscription 'Meine Ehre heißt Treuel' (my honour is called loyalty). (CP)

3. German Gold Cross that belonged to Harry Hermann, commander of 1./FJR 7, before it was passed to Harald Mors in September 1943. (HL)

4. Waffen SS runes. (CP)

5. A paratrooper equipped with ammunition cartridges for the brand new FG 42 sub-machine gun. (EQ)

that he'd been through. His eyes spoke more than his words: his people had overthrown him, and his close collaborators and supporters were against him. He was unshaven and was wearing a black coat over a dark blue suit, with a hat which partly covered his face.[5] The man who stood before me had been the leader of the Italian government for twenty years.

He was unrecognisable compared to the first time I had seen him. It was in Rome, in 1937. I had been part of the German delegation which attended the celebration events following victory in the Ethiopia campaign.

5   The impression Mussolini gave to his liberators was far from being that of a charismatic leader. Bosshammer recalls he 'wore a black coat and hat, and his face was pale. My impression of him was that of a man whose will was wavering, [he was] sick, exhausted, insecure, far from his glorious former persona.' Hoelscher confirms: 'I had the impression that I was facing a sick and exhausted man; not exactly the view I had of *il Duce* of Italy.' Gerlach also remembered similar feelings after his encounter with Mussolini: 'Confusion reigned in the room where *il Duce* was held. I found him pale and unshaven, with a few days beard growth, sitting on a bed. However, he welcomed me with a smile and shook my hand when I approached him.'

During the parade along the via del Imperio, I was a few steps away from
the tribune of honour, where Mussolini was: proud, self-confident, and at
the height of his fame and success. This was nothing like the Mussolini at
the Campo Imperatore. I felt sorry for this man, who would once again
be sent back to the war, to the world. He had been rescued by German
soldiers, not by his own compatriots. The latter had made him a prisoner.
You could not avoid this fact. Had I done a good job? I had some doubts...
But photographers soon arrived because they wanted us to leave the hotel
as the light was better outside. I informed Mussolini, and he told me dryly
in German '*Macht mit mir was ihr wollt!*' (Do what you want with me!).
This man knew that even though he had been liberated, he had not gained
his freedom or autonomy. Shortly afterwards he asked me a favour, and
I was willing to help him as much as I could. 'I beg you', he told me, 'set
my guards free. They have been kind to me.' Since the plan had always
been that no prisoners would be taken and that the Italians would be left
at the hotel, I guaranteed that this would be the case. He thanked me with
a nod of his head, but also with an absent gesture... As we got closer to
the aeroplane, his people surrounded him and greeted him in the Roman

The head of the paratroop company which landed on the Gran Sasso, Oberleutnant Georg
von Berlepsch, leaves the hotel. Two paratroopers guard the entrance (the one on the right
is armed with an FG 42). (EC)

(*Left*) Nicolás Hoelscher was a paratrooper in l./FJR 7. Apart from his participation in the Gran Sasso raid, he also fought at Anzio-Nettuno. He was captured on 30 August 1944 in the outskirts of Marines/Meulan, while defending Paris. After two years as a prisoner in the USA and France, he settled in Spain, and died on 3 May 2001. (FH)

(*Right*) Mors and von Berlepsch at the cable car station in Campo Imperatore at 14:25. To Mors' right is Oblt. Karl Schulze (with helmet), and to the left is Oblt. Hans Joachim Kurth. Next to him is Fieldwebel Wächtler, Mors' translator. [EC]

style. These were the same people who, an hour before, had held him prisoner with the intention of prosecuting him or handing him over to the Allies.

While this meeting was taking place, Captain Gerlach landed on the small terrace in front of the hotel. A platoon from the company's first section and the glider pilots had been ordered to prepare a runway. To do this they cleared the area of stones, and signaled it by marking out a swastika using sheets and tablecloths. The landing was perfect. Heinrich Gerlach recalls:

...As I stopped the engine and jumped out of the cab, a new thought came into my mind: How would I take off again from here? I called over to the man who had marked the landing area for me – Leutnant Meyer-Wehner – and asked: 'Do you have him?' He answered straightaway: 'Yes, we have him upstairs', and pointed at the second floor of the building. I ran and found the entrance to the building. Heavily armed paratroopers showed me where *il Duce*'s room was. Other paratroopers were in charge of disarming the Italians (...) Once I had left the room and was heading back to the aeroplane, Skorzeny suddenly approached me and asked me to take him to Pratica de Mare. I refused, telling him that I wasn't even sure myself how we would take off.

The difficulties with the take-off also seemed to worry Gerlach:

I ran towards my Storch, which I had left in the care of several paratroopers. The significant question was how I would be able to take off again. Doing it against the wind, as was normal, seemed too risky to me, especially as the take-off would need to be done facing the Gran Sasso mountain range and it was too steep. I decided to take off with the tail wind, which was also very risky. This option was more reasonable, despite the fact that there was a gap at the end of my 'runway'.

1. Waffen SS ring. This, as many others, was a particular item of clothing and not subject to any regulations. (CP)

2. Heavily armed paratroopers from 1st Company casually pose for the reporter Von Kayser. (EC)

3. Hauptmann Heinrich Gerlach, General Kurt Student's personal pilot, poses after being awarded the Knight's Cross.

4. Nicolas (Claus) Hoelscher photographed at the cable car station, immediately after the operation. He is the third one on the right. (FH)

5. German gliders near the hotel. In the foreground is Number 9, which carried Gerhard Opel's squad. In the background, from left to right, Number 6 (the one Skorzeny landed in) and Numbers 7 and 10. (EC)

10

Skorzeny Enters the Scene

As Gerlach meditated on these matters, and as he tried to persuade the exultant group of soldiers, paratroopers and Italians to leave the Gran Sasso as soon as possible, Skorzeny approached him again and

> ...begged me once more to take him with me. I again rejected his request. He kept on begging me using a whole manner of arguments, and I finally decided that Oberfeldwebel Hundt would come up and go with him, but I learned over the radio that his aeroplane had broken down. Skorzeny tormented me again with his pleas and once again I refused, arguing that the Storch had only two seats. Besides, he was too heavy (at least 100 kg) for the journey. I told him that one of his shortest officers should accompany Mussolini, but he said no. He wanted to accompany *il Duce* himself. He kept on begging me. Time was pressing on, and with it the danger of a possible English or American counter-attack. The Italians could have told them about our rescue operation, meaning we had to leave the place as

Mussolini poses next to the Germans and Italians. From left to right: Skorzeny, Schulze, Mussolini (behind him, General Soleti), Otto Scherdt, Meyer-Wehner, Faiola (with service cap), Karl Radl (Skorzeny's assistant), and two men from his team. (B)

Mussolini seen talking to Inspector Giuseppe Gueli, Moments before boarding the Fi-156 aeroplane. On the right is the war correspondent, Bruno von Kayser. (EC)

> quickly as possible. I finally agreed to Szkorzeny's pleas, who was almost on his knees by this time. I expressly informed him that the take-off would be extremely risky due to his size, but he didn't care at all; all he wanted was to come with us.

Gerlach had no explicit orders to take off from the Gran Sasso with Mussolini, but he decided to take the risk. Different versions of this event exist and Mors also recalls:

> I spoke with Gerlach, who had already positioned the aeroplane for take-off. He was thinking of transporting the two of them (Skorzeny and Mussolini) on the two-seater plane, although he preferred to have *il Duce* on his own. However, the second Storch had broken down and was unable to fly. Student had expressly ordered that Mussolini should be accompanied. I suggested he fly to the valley and take the two passengers there. As the pilot, the responsibility was his. Time was running out and he decided to take off from the mountain. Skorzeny climbed in first, and had to bend over behind the passenger seat. Then it was Mussolini's turn to climb aboard. He looked somewhat helpless...someone fastened his seat belt.

Lufwaffe ski cap (Bergmütze). This is identical to the one worn by Mors during the operation (CP).

Did Skorzeny pull rank over Gerlach? Despite the fact that both men held the rank of captain, regulations declared that an order from the SS outweighed any others. In an interview given after the war to the historian Arribo Petacco, Gerlach descibed how Skorzeny asked him to take him with him, implying that 'you must take care of the equipment and you never know...Something may go wrong....' Did he convince him? He certainly threatened him. The fact is that Skorzeny was representing Hitler and did not want to miss out on any glory that the company – in which he had undoubtedly participated – might achieve. The cunning Skorzeny wanted to return and tell Hitler that *he* had been the one to free *il Duce*.

As mentioned earlier, Student and Mors were happy to let Skorzeny accompany Mussolini to Germany once he had been liberated, and did not consider this to be a problem while they were planning the operation. Harald Mors had now fulfilled his mission and recalls:

> Someone had to accompany Mussolini, and Skorzeny seemed the right person to me. Taking into account the delicate military situation at the time (the Italian armistice, the Allied landing in Calabria and Salerno), we needed all of our officers. So, when Skorzeny volunteered to accompany Mussolini, I did not object. He was a policeman, wasn't he? The ideal person to carry out this mission... Naturally, I could not have foreseen that Skorzeny would take advantage of my trust and take credit for the operation. Or let it be attributed to him...

Mussolini approached the Storch, though not without expressing some reservations, asking, 'Couldn't we travel by land?'

The paratroopers looked on in astonishment: 'To our surprise, Skorzeny also climbed into the aeroplane, even though it only had two seats', recalled Bosshammer. Fifteen soldiers, German and Italian, helped Gerlach to take off, holding the plane by its wings. With a tailwind and hardly any terrain,

From left to right: Harald Mors, Karl Shulze, Feldwebel Eugen Abel (between the two and barely visible), Mussolini, General Soleti and Untersturmführer Otto Schwerdt. Behind is Uffz. Gedenk, the glider pilot. On the far left is Alberto Faiola, one of those charged with guarding Mussolini during his time in the Gran Sasso. (EC)

Gerlach gave the engine maximum power so as to create a catapult effect. The take-off was dramatic, as the plane fell down into the gap a few metres ahead. However the fall increased the speed, causing it to rise, and thanks to Gerlach's skill the manoeuvre was successful. The plane gained altitude, flew over the group of soldiers and headed west. Mors contacted Student's headquarters: 'Mission accomplished, *il Duce* has departed.'

Waffen SS officers' cap. (CP)

After flying for an hour, the Storch arrived at Pratica di Mare airfield, landing next to the He-111 plane that was waiting for Mussolini. The passengers disembarked and once they were on land, headed over to the Heinkel. Student had sent an officer to wait there for them, as planned, but Skorzeny quickly cut him off saying that he was now in charge. Gerlach continues:

> Mussolini called out to me and asked my name before getting into the "belly" of the plane. He shook my hand and with his usual hoarse voice, told me in rudimentary German: 'Captain, I owe you my life'. The Heinkel took off at once. I received a call from Student and told him that Mussolini was already flying towards Germany and that I would report to him immediately in person.

The Fieseler "Storch" Fi 156 pilot, Heinrich Gerlach, seen on the left, discusses the take-off with Skorzeny. Both photographs reflect the tension between the two men. Gerlach is wearing the Iron Cross 1st Class on his chest. (EC).

(*Above*) There was still time to pose for a photograph before boarding. From left to right: Skorzeny, Mors, Schwerdt (behind Mussolini), Obersturmführer Karl Radl (Skorzeny's assistant, with helmet), Stabsfeldwebel Alois Ehrmann and Inspector Giuseppe Gueli. (EC)

(*Left*) Mientras Gerlach lights a cigarette, while Skorzeny appears to be arguing with his subordinate, a fellow Austrian SS offcier, Robert Warger. Meanwhile, Von Berlepsch watches the scene quitley. Skorzeny's personal weapon is a Walther PPK. (EC)

(*Left*) M38 Paratrooper helmet, camouflaged for operations in the Mediterranean. The glider pilots used this model in the Gran Sasso raid. (CP)

(*Right*) A German MP 38 sub-machine gun. (CP)

Meanwhile, back at the Gran Sasso, the evacuation of the hotel had begun. It was at this moment that Harald Mors understood the importance of the action, its exceptional nature, and the audacity with which the mission had been planned.

> It seemed pointless to me that German soldiers had to die for this "finished" man. It soon became clear that Hitler thought differently. No one had forgotten the eleven paratroopers who had fallen just three days earlier in the operation against the *'Piacenza'* division.

After destroying the Italians' weapons, rescuing the glider panels and destroying the rest (evacuating the gliders was an impossible task, as there were no roads descending from the Gran Sasso), the soldiers left Campo Imperatore. As for the second Storch, which had been damaged in Assergi, it was able to take off again in the late afternoon once the damaged caused during its landing had been repaired. It took two hours for the last German soldier to leave Campo Imperatore. Given the fatigue accumulated by all of the troops over the previous twenty-four hours, Mors decided the battalion should encamp at the cable car station in Assergi, in an area near the river, and close to the road.[6] The next day they set off on their return journey to Frascati.

---

6   One of the participants in the operation, Hans Kohlrautz, an Oberjäger from 1st Company, remembered an interesting detail. After the evacuation of Campo Imperatore, he and Karl Sitzberger went to requisition blankets from a nearby manor house in Assergi. When they were in the hall they heard the the sound of a radio coming from the attic. They went upstairs quietly so that the staff didn't have time to notice their presence, or turn off the radio. They learned that the Italian government had reached an agreement with the British for an aeroplane to land at the hotel the following day, 13 September, and take Mussolini. According to Kohlrautz, who died in December 2002, Mors knew they had found a radio, but not about the English rescue plan...

11

Surprise at the Gran Sasso?

The quick but determined preparation of the attack gravitated toward the element of surprise. However, neither Mors' paratroopers nor the SS commandos knew what was waiting for them on the summit of the Gran Sasso. Perhaps the Italian intelligence services (Servizio Informazioni Militari – SIM) worked better than the Germans had previously thought.

Since 26 August, a guard of forty-three carabinieri and thirty policemen, with two heavy machine guns and two light machine guns had been ready at the Hotel Campo Imperatore, as well as a unit with six guard dogs. In a typically Italian act, the cast of those on guard at the Gran Sasso was mixed: carabinieri and policemen, and such a duplicity of command would complicate any decision making.

From left to right, Lentz (with machine gun ammunition), unknown (with cartridges for the FG 42 sub-machine gun), Müth (with Kar 98 rifle equipped with grenade launcher), Keller (with a Leica camera), Heinz Karrenbrock (with gunbelt with flares and a Kodak Retina camera), Jupp Vieth (with FG 42 sub-machine gun) and Heinz Kubitschke, who died in February 1944.

Mussolini on his way to the Fi.156. Behind him is SS Sub-Lieutenant Otto Schwerdt. (S)

After being transferred by seaplane from La Maddalena to Lake Bracciano[7], and after a trip – again – by ambulance, Mussolini arrived in Assergi on 2 September and was temporarily installed in the Villa Mascitelli, in Fonte Cerreto, at the foot of the Gran Sasso. Giuseppe Gueli, Inspector General of Public Security in Trieste, was in charge of the dictator's custody, and had almost an implicit authorisation allowing him to dispose of the prisoner for an eventual transfer. However, he had to coordinate everything with Lieutenant Faiola, who, although very hostile toward the English (of whom he had been a prisoner in Tobruk), was more dependent on the directives of the Badoglio government. Indeed, he had confided Gueli that he 'had prepared everything so that *il Duce* would not to fall into enemy hands'.

Alberto Faiola had been made responsible for *il Duce*'s custody on 9 August, after replacing Colonel Meoli. Under his command were the carabinieri and policemen who were in charge of the surveillance of Villa Weber, which served as a prison for Mussolini on the island of Magdalena. He was accompanied by the general of the police of the Supreme Command, Francesco Saverio Pòlito. Faiola had received clear instructions from his immediate superior, Commander Cerica: in case of an enemy attack, he was to defend the position at all costs and request reinforcements from the Navy Command. On the day of his appointment he also met Badoglio, who gave him 'his own instructions' about what was to happen to *il Duce* in the event of a rescue attempt. They had also met Pòlito: 'Badoglio', he writes 'had given me orders to kill him'.

---

7   Luck was on Student's side: A German seaplane squadron, prepared for the hypothetical release of Mussolini, was stationed at Lake Bracciano. The commander informed Student that after a false alarm, a white seaplane landed and that an ambulance later left for an unknown destination. This information motivated the decision to send Dr Krutoff to inspect the area surrounding the Gran Sasso.

1. Toni Schneiders, photographed in 1943, was one of the war reporters who filmed and photographed Mussolini's rescue. (B)

2. M 40 helmet with Waffen SS insignia. (CP)

3. A Waffen SS eagle in BeVo fabric. (CP)

4. The Fi-156 "Storch" ready for take-off to Pratica di Mare, Rome. (COG)

However, La Magdalena had become an unsafe place, and the decision to move Mussolini took place in Rome after General Basso, commander of the Sardinian forces, wrote a letter to Minister Sorice. In turn, Pòlito confirmed this need after being sent to the island by the police chief, Senise.

The former was in charge of choosing a new destination for the prisoner, but had a car accident after he had found him. This meant that Senise was replaced by Inspector Genral Gueli, a man defined as 'an official of exceptional professional qualities'. Gueli suggested the transfer to the Gran Sasso after verifying that 'there were no German troops in the area'.

Gueli's attitude towards *il Duce* was more like that of a benevolent protector rather than a strict prison guard. If it had been necessary to murder Mussolini, just as the orders had instructed, he would not have sent his own men. This was something he had decided on the same night as his encounter with Badoglio: despite having given him his word, 'as luck had been favourable to me, among the millions of Italians loyal to *il Duce*, I decided to do everything possible to save him.' He was the one who informed Mussolini of all the events that were taking place abroad, and was also the one who confirmed in front of Badoglio, who favoured moving the prisoner to a safer place, that Campo Imperatore was an 'impregnable fortress'. His management of security was very relaxed, ordering any automatic weapons and ammunition to be locked away. The guard dogs were positioned in the most unlikely areas of attack. Anyone else in his position, with such a minimum amount of experience, would have done more and better. Gueli recalls:

> As I expected a German coup d'état at Campo Imperatore, and in the hope of encouraging one, I ensured the surveillance was very relaxed:
>
> 1. The men had no specialist training, and were typically agents who had come from Trieste with me. They did not understand what was going on and thought they were on holiday.
> 2. Automatic weapons were stored under lock and key.
> 3. Ammunition was also stored in a locked room (they wasn't much, but I didn't bother asking for more).
> 4. The guard dogs were chained up in the building's blind spots.

On the very same morning of the 12th, the prefect of L'Aquila, Rodolfo Biancorosso, telephoned Gueli. He wanted to have a private conversation, as he was worried the lines might have been tapped. He arranged to meet him at the bottom of the cable car. The prefect was convinced that the Germans were going to attack the Gran Sasso, and advised Gueli to transfer Mussolini. Gueli did not think this was necessary, but when he returned to the hotel, he was told by the ski instructor, Domenico Antonelli, that the civillian staff and those operating the cable cars were already in a state of alarm. Gueli did not wish to comment on the disturbance to Faiola in case he 'reinforced the surveillance'.

He waited all morning for instructions from Rome, orders that would not arrive as Mors' men had cut off all communications thus isolating the hotel. At 13.30 – half an hour before the attack – police chief Carmine Senise telephoned Gueli and

1 & 2. Toni Schneiders seen by the cable car during the evacuation of Campo Imperatore. The films for his camera are in the breast pocket of his jump jacket. The paratrooper to his left is holding several FG 42 sub-machine guns. (EC)

3. Bruno von Kayser was the war reporter for the Gran Sasso raid, not to mention a European ballroom dancing champion both before and after the war. He would also take part in the final German parachute jump in the Ardennes, in December 1944. (COG)

4. The final moments before the Fi-156 takes off. The pilot, Gerlach, can be seen in the cockpit. Mussolini's silhouette and Skorzeny's head are also visible. Next to the plane are (left to right), Elmar Mayer-Wehner, Karl Radl and Otto Schwerdt. Toni Schneiders (with helmet) can be seen filming. He has with him the camera case that, as he told the author, he would carry throughout war until he was wounded near Paris. Next to him, bending down and taking photographs, is Bruno von Kayser. (COG, via Schneiders)

read out the following telegram from Rome (where German troops were already engaged in combat): 'Maximum caution recommended to Inspector Gueli. Those orders received beforehand are confirmed and remain valid.' What did this mean? Mussolini should not be handed over to the Germans? Should he be executed in case of any attempt to liberate him? On Saturday afternoon, Mussolini had been caught threatening to kill himself with a razor blade, although his actions had been rather elaborate and with no thought of the practical consequences involved. In addition to this, he had previously asked Faiola for a gun so that he could commit suicide, an act that Faiola remembered in a report from January 1945:

> While listening to the radio on the afternoon of 10 December, Mussolini learned that, among the other clauses of the armistice, he was to be turned over to the enemy. This had such an impact on him that he called me during the night and told me he would rather take his own life than fall into enemy hands. I assured him we had received no orders to hand him over, and I promised and swore that whatever happened we would protect him, and help him escape through the mountains. Only then did he calm down. However, it was only temporary as he got up again during the night and began to pace nervously around his room.

Did he really intend to take his own life? Or was he just making it clear that he was not prepared to be taken alive by the enemy? What did the order mean? Intensify the surveillance or safeguard Mussolini's life? Gueli chose in favour of the second option, and likewise persuaded Faiola and the person in direct charge of *il Duce*'s surveillance, Second Lieutenant Osvaldo Antichi. Later, during lunch, Gueli and Faiola agreed that, in case of emergency, they would not use weapons: 'During the meal we talked of the eventuality of a German intervention. We both agreed that we would surrender without any resistance'. The two would follow Mussolini to Germany.

12

Skorzeny's Version of Events

There are several exaggerations and mistakes in the version of events given by Skorzeny. On the one hand, he asserts that during the preparatory meeting of 11 September it was said that it would take three days to bring the gliders from France. This is not true, since they were already on Italian soil, in Grosetto. The *III./Luflandegeschwaser 1*, consisting of 32 *Henschel 126*s and 120 DFS-230 gliders, had departed from its base in Valences (France) on 8 September at 08:56 (as stated in the report by the squadron's commander, Oberleutnant Heidenreich), and arrived in Grosetto at 17:58. Other elements from the unit joined the following day, on 9 September.

The Austrian also comments that he was authorised to take with him all the men he wanted, in addition to ninety paratroopers. According to his version, the departure was to be at 19:00. However, why leave at that time if Pratica di Mare is only a little over 100 km from Campo Imperatore? Skorzeny seems to have forgotten the coordination that needed to exist between the airborne group and the the troops on the ground. How would the latter have been able to reach

A Fallschirmjäger carrying a pistol fires a flare next to one of the gliders used in the rescue. (EC)

the cable car station, and thus protect the airborne group, if it had been on its way since 03:00?

Skorzeny describes how he spent the night prior to the action studying the flight direction, the formation of the gliders, the landing procedures, etc. Such details would have been closely guarded at Luftwaffe General Headquarters. Nor does he mention anything, at this point, about the ground column:

> We wanted to catch the Italians by surprise with a risky, though by no means desparate, plan. We had experience, especially after having carried out an attack similar to the one at the Gran Sasso in Ebgen Emael (Belgium), in 1940. It was four minutes before the Belgian soldiers first opened fire against the German paratroopers. We tried to imitate exactly the rhythm and the style of this operation. Besides, we had with us an Italian general who was to be the first to descend so that the Italian garrison would not be alarmed. We were well-armed: we had machine guns, sub-machine guns and grenades.

Luftwaffe paratrooper's cloth badge. (COG)

Another view of the DFS-230 glider flown by Meyer-Wehner. (EC)

As for the gliders, according to the Austrian there was a delay in their arrival: they arrived at Pratica de Mare at 11:00, so Student himself would have suggested a delay of 24 hours. Why do this, if the useful time margin had not been affected? What would the ground column troops, which Skorzeny has still forgotten about, have done in this case? Would they simply have received the order to retreat by radio?

Continuing with his account, Skorzeny says that after midday, Allied bombers flew over the airfield. After this attack, '…the only concerns came from the craters generated by the bombs. Indeed, two gliders were unable to take off as a result.' This tale is also a fantasy as while it is true that an Allied formation flew over the airfield, it did not drop any bombs. Its target was completey different. No explosion or craters appeared on the runway, and no glider was grounded for this reason – a fact that all veterans consulted by this author have confirmed.

To begin with, according to Skorzeny, and here he moves significantly away from all other versions of events, twelve gliders were to land on the Gran Sasso, guided in formation by the same pilot who had taken himself and Radl on the

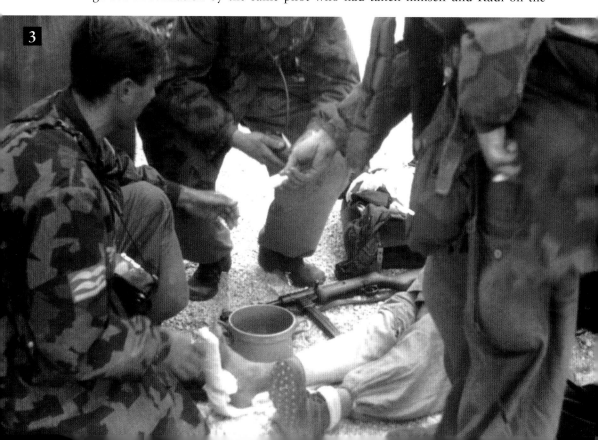

1. A German paratrooper's jump boots. (CP)

2. Luftwaffe Pilot- Observer badge, with BSW markings. (CP)

3. Dr Otto Brunner, bending down on the left, assists SS Obersturmführer Ulli Menzel, who was wounded during the landing. Note that Menzel's weapon is an MP 41 sub-machine gun. (EC)

4. SS soldiers near the Assergi cable car station after leaving Campo Imperatore. Sitting on the chair is Untersturmführer Schwerdt and on the right is Obersturmführer Uli Menzel, who was wounded during the landing. (EQ)

5. Several wounded paratroopers, laid out on a truck, are being tended to in Assergi. (EC)

reconnaissance flight to take photographs over the hotel (according to Student, Skorzeny 'only travelled as a passenger on the reconnaissance flight'). The twenty men in the first gliders had to protect the landing of the third plane, which had Skorzeny, Warger and Soleti onboard. Radl might have been on the fourth. The alleged shower of Allied bombs could have delayed the departure, in the same way as two gliders – those that had to preceed Skorzeny's – had to remain on the ground. Thus the third glider, the one containing Skorzeny, had to be the one to lead the mission, and would be without an escort at the time of landing on the Gran Sasso. It was a case of 'force majeure' that "forced" him to take command: once the leading gliders could not fly, Skorzeny had no choice but to lead the formation.

As previously mentioned, Skorzeny also contradicts the official order of the formation (*Kette*) of gliders and Henschels. Upon reaching the target, he ordered the pilot to dive down, not wanting to miss the opportunity to land on the small area of ground available. Student had ordered that if a proper landing was not possible, then the gliders should attempt to fly up to the Assergi Valley. Whatever the case, diving was strictly forbidden. Skorzeny directly disobeyed this order. He wanted to be the first on the Gran Sasso and so he pulled rank (however, as a 'guest', he had no authority in the operation), and ordered the pilot to dive, jeopardising the entire operation.

He describes the liberation of Mussolini as follows:

I passed a carabinieri on guard, who was caught completely by surprise, and entered a room outside the complex, where a telegrapher was writing down a transmission. With a blow I knocked him off his chair and destroyed the radio with the butt of my rifle. Back outside, I climbed 25 metres up an embankment and tried to reach the top. I saw an unmistakable shaved head appear from a window: Mussolini. I shouted at him to stay inside and headed towards the entrance. The carabinieri on guard wore surprised expressions, but before they could react, my men had opened fire with their sub-machine guns. Meanwhile, Soleti shouted in Italian 'Don't shoot! Don't shoot!', which only contributed to the growing confusion. I forced my way through the soldiers (since we were too close to open fire), climbed the stairs and knocked on a door, behind which were Mussolini and two officers. Behind me stood Untersturmfürer Schwerdt, while through the window appeared the heads of two SS men who had climbed over the wall. We neutralised the two Italians and *il Duce* remained in the custody of Schwerdt. We left the room, not without having first seen my assistant, Radl, who said he had everything under control. Three other gliders had crash landed, while a fourth had been smashed into a thousand pieces. I could not wait for reinforcements. I played wisely and requested an unconditional surrender. An Italian colonel appeared before me with a glass of red wine to toast, 'To the winners!'

1

This narration turns the operation into something of an adventure, with all the necessary ingredients to make one believe that Skorzeny was - as he was later defined – 'the most dangerous man in Germany'. The "colonel" story is rather mysterious. The highest ranking officer was the aforementioned carabinieri lieutenant, Alberto Faiola, and the police official, Giuseppe Gueli. There is no mention of a "colonel" at all. As for the crashed gliders, only Skorzeny was the one to see them. When the gliders appeared near the hotel, Gueli, like Mussolini, approached the window. When the paratroopers left the gliders they were greeted by a group of Italians with a bottle of wine (as described by Skorzeny). There were no shots fired - although, in truth, there was one: the 'accidental' one that had been fired by Irrgang - and no one else heard the machine gun fire that Skorzeny refers to.

Mors commented on Skorzenhy's version of events as follows:

It is not about repairing old wounds, because anyone can see Skorzeny's unscrupulous, selfish and disloyal behaviour. To deny his achievements in the preliminary phase of the mission and investigations would be unjust, but on the other hand, it is also true that any layman in military matters may also understand that such a delicate and complex action as the liberation of Mussolini, which required maximum collaboration between airborne and

1. Insignia worn on Waffen SS combat jackets. (CP)

2. Luftwaffe pilot's ring. (HL)

3. Ronsdorf, pilot of glider Number 8, was wounded during the landing and is being assisted here by his partner, Gedenk and an Italian soldier. (EQ)

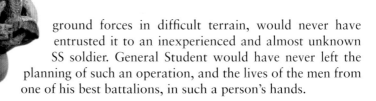

ground forces in difficult terrain, would never have entrusted it to an inexperienced and almost unknown SS soldier. General Student would have never left the planning of such an operation, and the lives of the men from one of his best battalions, in such a person's hands.

Nicolás Hoelscher also presents a similar argument, dismantling the theory that it was Skorzeny who planned the attack:

In 1943, the Waffen-SS did not have resources to liberate Mussolini, as only the Luftwaffe had paratroopers, gliders and tow planes. The operation was planned and developed with the upmost precision. No heroic gestures would be required on the Gran Sasso. It is true that Skorzeny fully completed his mission to find the whereabouts of *il Duce*; an integral foundation of the operation. However, it is also true that Skorzeny at no time had any command over our Fallschirmjäger battalion, whose leader was Harald Mors.

The aforementioned Italian historian, Arrigo Pettaco, declared at the congress held in 1993 that Skorzeny was, 'undoubtedly a braggart, the kind of man who in peace time might be a criminal, but in war time became a hero. Such things happen often.'

The story of this operation, which is confusing and intriguing in itself, has been obscured by the personal vanity of Skorzeny who invented many "facts" about what took place.

1. Ronsdorf's glider pilot ring, which was found in 2010 in the same place where he crash landed. (MD)

2. Dr Otto Brunner, the Austrian Medical Officer who travelled in 1st Company's glider. He died in April 2008. (EC)

3. View of Campo Imperatore from where Uffz. Ronsdorf landed. (MD)

4. German propaganda was in charge of spreading the tale of the Gran Sasso raid. This Dutch publication from 1943, entitled 'The Liberation of Mussolini', clearly depicts the operation on the front cover. (COG)

5. In the Italian operations in September 1943, the FG 42 (Fallschirmjägergewehr 42) was used for first time. This was a light rifle that used a powerful 7.9 mm cartridge. Around 7,000 units of this revolutionary weapon, specifically designed for paratroopers, were manufactured, but was later overshadowed by the MP 44 sub-machine gun. (B)

6. Knee pads specifically designed for the Fallschirmjäger. (CP)

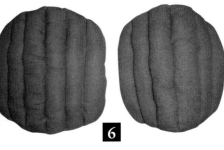

13

"My Dear Mors: I Don't Want Any Trouble With Himmler"

On the morning of 14 September, a group of soldiers and officers came running to the battalion commander's tent. The 07:00 radio bulletin was broadcasting the voice of 'Mussolini's liberator': Otto Skorzeny. From the microphone of Berlin Radio he had proclaimed himself as the planner and commander of the operation. By inventing "facts", he emphasised that the role played by the paratroopers was insignificant, even saying that at least a third of the paratroopers involved - thus around 100 - had died after crashing into the rocks.

Von Berlepsch was literally out of his mind and demanded, along with the rest of the unit, a statement of rectification. Mors went to the General Headquarters and informed Student, demanding that the truth be told and for the soldiers' families to be informed of what had happened, who according to the news bulletin, might otherwise believe that their relatives were dead. Student was not as angry as Mors. At the time, Mussolini's liberation was not a major priority for him as his mind was preoccupied with bigger matters: the occupation of Rome. However, he tried to calm Mors down by assuring him that he would speak to Hitler personally in the coming days.

Mussolini and Hitler during the time when no one dared to doubt the power of their alliance.

What had happened? A new mistake by the paratroopers or Student? Maybe Göring had been overconfident? Student had told him about the operation's success and he wanted to verify it with his own eyes, personally going to wait for *il Duce* at the airport in Vienna. On the stopover in Vienna, after arriving at the Imperial hotel where he was staying, Skorzeny immediately telephoned Obergruppenführer Ernst Kaltenbrunner, an Austrian like himself, and the head of the *Reichssicherheitshauptant* (Reich Main Security Office), telling him in full detail what had happened on the mountain. There was a strong relationship between both men, and Skorzeny was certainly playing two sides, working for both Hitler and for Kaltenbrunner. In all this, the 'Austrian mafia' played a leading role. The matter was in the hands of the Nazi chiefs, who were eager for propaganda and at odds with

Commander Harald Mors during the ceremony where Student awarded him with the German Gold Cross (DKG), on 28 September 1943.

each other. Himmler immediately called Hitler, telling him the great success by the SS, led by Skorzeny. Himmler telephoned Skorzeny again, telling him that Hitler would be there to meet himself and Mussolini in Munich. The Führer would award him with the *Ritterkreuz* (Knight's Cross of the Iron Cross), but this was not enough. The telephone rang again. This time it was Hitler, who wanted to speak with Skorzeny: 'Commander Skorzeny, you have successfully completed our mission. Your Führer thanks you.' He was also told about his promotion to Sturmbannführer.

Skorzeny and Mussolini arrived in Munich in a Ju 52, where they were received by a delighted Hitler. Days later, Skorzeny would speak at the Sports Palace in Berlin, surrounded by the main Nazi commanders, and in front of a cheering crowd.

Skorzeny was declared a hero of Nazi Germany, and as an intrepid soldier by the Allies. The irony of fate was that this was all due to the only endeavour of his fearless career that he did not plan or in which he was the main protagonist. For German propaganda, it was convenient at this stage of the war to maintain the high morale of the army with such an example of efficiency, decision-making and audacity: the exceptional assault on the Gran Sasso was down to a man of extraordinary ability.

However, could Student obtain a rectification directly from the Führer? Although he wanted to correct the wrong information about the operation as quickly as possible, the general was unable keep his promise. He spoke with Göring, telling him in detail of how *il Duce*'s liberation really took place. But there was no turning back, and besides, Hitler had already awarded him the *Ritterkreuz*. Thanks to this recognition, Hitler had accepted Skorzeny's version of events as valid. Himmler had beaten Göring, the Luftwaffe and the paratroopers. There was no love lost between the supreme commander of the Luftwaffe and the Reichsführer, and Himmler knew to take advantage of this rivalry by exaggerating the merits of his own men to the detriment of the Fallschirmjäger. Student accepted this and responded to an insisting Mors: 'Dear Mors, I don't want any trouble with Himmler.' Student answered in the same tone to the petition to rectify the situation, saying that no paratrooper had fallen during the assault. And so the matter was settled. But Mors was not satisfied. On a trip to Berlin at the beginning of October, he expressed a complaint about it to the Luftwaffe Headquarters. However, Mors' attempts were cut short when he received a telegram from the Führer's headquarters stating that: 'The Führer himself has ordered that the news be spread in this way to show the world that he was willing to sacrifice the blood of the best German soldiers for his friend Mussolini.' The propaganda had won.

1. Luftwaffe penknife with SMF markings. (CP)

2. Hauptmann Gerlach (left) and Leutnant Meyer-Wehner, Skorzeny's glider pilot, after being decorated with the Knight's Cross. (DA)

3. At Lake Nemi, on 28 September 1943, Student decorated those involved in the operation. Elimar Meyer-Wehner was given the Knight's Cross, while Harald Mors and Gerhard Langguth (foreground) were given the German Cross in Gold. Three glider pilots, Heiner Lohrmann, Hans Neelmeyer and Gustav Thielmann also received this award. Von Berlepsch received the German Cross in Gold a few days later as he was still convalescing. (DA)

4. From left to right, Bernd Boshammer, Romano Mussolini (Benito Mussolini's son, who died in 2006) and Harald Mors. The photograph was taken in 1993 at a ceremony in Assergi celebrating the 50th anniversary of the operation. (COG)

Mors says:

Skorzeny named one of his reports 'My Mussolini Adventure'. This is a suitable expression because for him, this was all it was; he had no responsibilities, no orders to give, no objectives to achieve. For our soldiers it was not an adventure, but a very serious military action. He was a commander in charge of his own men and had received orders to follow. I had to reconcile two important factors: to reach the objective and protect my paratroopers. I did this without shouting and without taking any unnecessary risks that might bring me fame and glory. When Skorzeny and the SS claimed the honour and glory for the operation and I couldn't get a rectification, I promised my soldiers that when I left command of the battalion at the end of September, I would publicly clarify the matter when the war was over. I expected more than I received. The operation deserves to enter into history simply as an example of the courage displayed by the German soldiers. However, it has been stifled by propaganda and so much journalistic lightheartedness. It has been sacrificed by personal ambitions, rivalries, and a scandalous political class

1. The 'Signal' magazine's second November edition of 1943 (n° 22) included a photographic report on the liberation of Mussolini. In addition, it also produced a 4-page black and white special edition. (COG)

2. The Berenbold brigade in Luftwaffe tropical uniform, armed with an MP 40 machine gun and wearing a glider pilot badge on his chest.

3. Front page of the *Völkischer Beobachter* newspaper on 18 September 1943. The caption reports that Mussolini is seen leaving his confinement, accompanied by his liberators. This copy belonged to Leutnant Hans Joachim Kurth. (COG)

willing to see this through. These factors have covered up, but not destroyed, the determination, courage and capabilities of the paratroopers who carried out this difficult mission that had been assigned to them.

Mors was a military man who had fulfilled his mission perfectly. He had led a combined air and land operation, with a particularly difficult objective, but which had been deployed with perfect synchronicity. Such a task could only have been done by a professional. However, the operation to free Mussolini was not just a military matter, nor did it only have military consequences. Above all, it was political and Hitler himself understood it in this way. He clearly did not need Mussolini as a military leader, but as the founder of fascism. On the afternoon of 15 September, Mussolini announced that '...he resumed the leadership at the forefront of Fascism'. However, neither this declaration, nor the subsequent creation of the Social Republic of Italy, which in Hitler's words was an 'artificial creation', led to the genuine reestablishment of his leadership. Italy had abandoned him.

Hitler wanted to give a political and personal meaning to Mussolini's liberation and was determined that this fact was attributed to his representative, in particular, and the SS in general. Skorzeny was naturally a vain, sly man, but he understood what his Führer expected of him.

Skorzeny would always reject another account that wasn't his own. His attitude has always been contemptuous of Mors and of his version of events. As part of an

The column of Italian and German lorries used by the paratroopers gets ready to leave Assergi. (EC)

interview in 1973,[8] he was asked for his opinion on the vindication of Student's paratroopers and answered as follows:

> Speaking from memory does not help clarify a situation as time goes by. I was in Italy and was sent there by Hitler; that is not contradicted by anyone. All the German media in Italy supported me in that mission. Nobody says otherwise (...) Student provided men and aircraft with their corresponding commandos ...and so what? Where was Mors at 14:00 on Sunday, 12 September 1943? I'll tell you where: with the men at the bottom of the cable car. Who entered the hotel? Who entered Mussolini's room? Who made his guards surrender...? Fortunately, this has not been denied by anyone!
>
> The operation's notoriety, that has been personified in me by the media, annoyed the others. But that always happens (...). It is always personified in someone, and on this occasion it was my turn, for the simple reason that Hitler appointed me: I started it, I pursued it and I ended it, that is to say, with several helping hands.

What Skorzeny said is a clear example of 'savoir faire' [know how]. Embedded in the Nazi myth of being superman, he had known how to translate his beliefs

---

8   Broadcast on Solar (2003 and 2005). The author recalls how 'on one or two occasions he responded with a string of expletives in German and Spanish against those who slandered or contradicted him. However, in the narrative of Mussolini's liberation, Solar followed the "official" version, which historically assumed that 'Skorzeny and his commandos' were the real protagonists of the operation.

about the Gran Sasso into facts. Skorzeny's logic in claiming the role of being the main protagonist in Mussolini's liberation rests on a consequential relationship that is hard to break down unless analysed in depth: he had been charged by Hitler to find the place where Mussolini had been hidden; had participated in the aerial reconnaissance over Campo Imperatore; was part of the airborne command that assaulted the hotel; he had the highest rank, and was the first to introduce himself to *il Duce*, before taking him to Hitler. The party's armour and propaganda sounding board merely closed the circle.

Even the members of the SS recognised this. Eugen Dollman was Himmler's representative at the German embassy in Rome, and assistant to Field Marshal Kesselring. In his opinion, there was no doubt about the merit of the paratroopers.

> In my opinion, and also that of Field Marshal Kesselring, the real protagonists were General Student, General Commander Mors and Captain Gerlach. Skorzeny's role was to act as an advisor or better still, as a police observer, in the search for Mussolini. That was his mission. The sole responsibility for the military operation belonged to General Student. That the success of the operation was attributed to Skorzeny was something that surprised even Kesselring himself.
>
> I remember in 1959, a year before his death, the field marshal talked extensively with me about this matter. He repeated again that the person in charge of the mission had exclusively been Student and his paratroopers.

Soldbuch (military ID) beloning to Eric Czeka (3./FJR 7). (COG)

Fabric glider pilot's badge. (HL)

From Student's point of view:

The ownership of the military operation belongs to the one who drew up the plan and who led the troops to carry it out. Skorzeny had nothing to do with the plan. The military action was led by Commander Mors. He was in charge of liberating Mussolini. Skorzeny was a man endowed with great vitality, intelligence and courage, as well as being gifted with a powerful imagination, but he did not liberate Mussolini. Mors, on the other hand, was responsible for all of the paratroopers involved in the operation. If it had failed, Skorzeny would have been careful not to take responsibility. Rather, the names of Student and Mors would have been at the forefront. If I had personally commanded the paratroopers on the Gran Sasso - something that was not feasible – the 'Skorzeny myth' would never have existed.

On the other hand, even in the 1950s, Mors' words and attitude were not exactly ambiguous. According to him, it was clear enough that the action had been sacrificed due to personal ambitions, rivalries and political scandals:

A selection of Skorzeny's men being decorated at the Berlin Sports Palace on 3 October 1943. From right to left; Obersturmführer Ulrich Menzel, Untersturmführer Otto Schwerdt, Unterscharführer Hans Holzer, Untersturmführer Robert Warger, Hauptscharführer Manns and Unterscharführer Bernhard Cieslewitz. Menzel and Manns were awarded the German Cross in Gold. (B)

We had a different point of view. Among the paratroopers a fuse was lit that has never been completely extinguished. All of those involved in the operation saw a contempt for the paratroopers in Skorzeny's mannerisms. Some people went even further, openly stating that the day would come when the paratroopers would take revenge for this SS trap. I should have officially rejected these statements, but they understood me and I understood them.

The internal struggle was also experienced in other fields, as for example in the propaganda that came from Berlin, where the Luftwaffe openly stated that 'the paratroopers liberated Mussolini'. The general rivalry between the Luftwaffe and the SS was only increased by events at the Gran Sasso. We surely lack of a fair criterion for a correct assessment of this conflict, apart from being irrelevant nowadays. But it is different when we refer to Skorzeny and the Great Sasso. Surely we lack the right criterion for an accurate assessment of this confrontation, not to mention the fact that its is irrelevant now anyway. But it's different when referring to the Gran Sasso. If it was not enough then – and it seems to still be the same today – to obtain a fair assessment of the myth (which in my opinion is what is happening today: the same story, told in a slightly different way, is continually retold without any form of criticism), then a correct and accurate evaluation of the facts must be undertaken. This is the purpose behind my story...

Hopefully, Harald Mors' desire has now been fulfilled.

Skorzeny poses next to Adolf Hitler after he had awarded him the Knight's Cross of the Iron Cross. (CP)

A paratroop officer's jacket decorated with both Iron Crosses (1st and 2nd Class). Also visible is the Luftwaffe paratrooper badge and the Wound Badge in black. (CP)

Official Report of Oberleutnant Karl Schulze, commander of 3./FJR 7

In the official report by the commander of 3rd Company, an 'absence of heroes' in the operation is notable. The style of the report is a long way from Skorzeny's version of events. It was written on 15 September by Karl Schulze, who had been slightly injured three days before the operation, following the disarming of the Italian '*Piacenza*' Division.

On 11 September 1943, the company received the order to arrive in the town of Assergi as soon as possible the following day (12 September), crossing Monte Porzio, Valmontone, Ferentino, Sora, Capistrello and Castelvechio, and occupy the cable car station that connected the valley with the Gran Sasso, before meeting up with 1st Company, under the command of Oberleutnant Baron Georg von Berlepsch, who had been sent to the hotel to liberate *il Duce*.

Once the motorised column had passed, the road to L'Aquila was blocked. We had a section from the Panzer (anti-tank) Company with us. The battalion's top command had joined the company.

After the battalion commander had checked the road, the column set off at 03:00 on 12 September 1943. Another Company (2nd) had now been

added to 1st Company. The march was carried out under caution. A group of motorcyclists was sent as an advanced detachment under the command of Leutnant Weber. The company reached the turn off to Assergi at around 14:00, after a tiring march through the mountains and without having met any of the expected enemy resistance. The company arrived in Assergi shortly after the advanced detachment. When leaving the town, the detachment found a guard post. Some soldiers had already left and the head of the company remained under fire from the men who were posted in the houses. It was then decided that a group should go and search the houses to neutralise the shooters. The 2nd Section was in charge of reaching the cable car station in the valley. When it arrived, the station had already been occupied by the advanced detachment and the soldiers who were there were unarmed. By orders of the battalion commander, on the night of 13 September we camped in the town of Camarda. At 21:00 on the same day, 13 September, the company returned to the starting point: Frascati.

Karl Schulze,
Oberleutnant and Company Commander

Losses: None
Vehicles: 4 lorries, 1 motorcycle and 2 wagons

Order of Combat for I./FJR 7 in September 1943

The unit was given this name so as to 'camouflage' it. At the end of August 1943, it was in quartered in Frascati, and then transferred to the Albanian mountains on 2 September. It successfully participated in the disarming of the 103rd Italian Infantry Division in Albano-Genzano, as well as in the occupation of 111th Infantry Regiment's GHQ. All this took place on 9 September, three days before the Gran Sasso operation.

Major Harald Mors handed back command of the battalion to Major Harry Hermann on 30 September 1943, after he had recovered from an illness. In addition, the unit recovered its old name Fallschirmjäger Lehr Battalion.

Battalion Commanders	Major Harry Hermann (until 29/07/43)	
	Major Otto Harald Mors (from 01/08/43 until 30/09/43)	
Adjutant	Oberleutnant Hans Joachim Kurth	later, Leutnant Herold
Ordinance Offizier	Oberleutnant Alfred Romanskie	Oberleutnant Rolfs
	Oberleutnant Böger	
Nachrichten-Zug (Radio)	Leutnant Karl-Heinz Blumenthal	
Hauptfw	Feldwebel Herbert Ripke	
Stabskompanie	Oberleutnant Weber	Zahlm, Both
	Oberleutnant H. J. Kurth	Zahlm, Jung
	Oberzahlm Becker	Dr. Schulze
	Leutnant Lungwitz	Dr. Brunner
	Oberzahlm Schmidt	

1.Kompanie	Oberleutnant Georg Freiherr von Berlepsch (+ 2.02.44.) (replaced Oberleutnant Weiss)	
I.Zug (section)	Leutnant Joswig	Feldwebel Rahden
II.Zug	Feldwebel Eugen Abel	Feldwebel Alfred Asbach
III.Zug	Leutnant Hans Weber (+9.09.43) (replaced by Leutnant Gradler)	Feldwebel Matthias Heck
Spieß (Sergeant Major)	Hfw. Arnold Pic	Fw. Bernd Bosshammer
	Hfw. Dienstt	
2.Kompanie	Oberleutnant Hans Georg Fischer	
I.Zug	Leutnant Schmidt	Fw. Otto Pawelcyk
II.Zug	Leutnant Otterbein	Fw. Franz Kopp
III.Zug	Leutnant Herman Wollter	Fw. Erich Pliwischkies
Spieß	Hfw. Flöricke	
3.Kompanie	Oberleutnant Karl Schulze	
I.Zug	Leutnant Hahn	Stabsfeldwebel Alois Ehrmann
II.Zug	Leutnant Lücht	Leutnant Braun
III.Zug	Oberfeldwebel Schröder	Fw. Tremel, Fw. Schultz
Spieß	Hfw. Kleber	Hfw. Walter Schmidt
4.Kompanie	Hauptmann Lisowski	
I.Zug	Leutnant Keller	Fw. Lenhardt
II.Zug	Leutnant Opel	Fw. Bunte
III.Zug	Leutnant Ehrlich	Fw. Wolk
Spieß	Fw. Gerhard Kempe	

The Protagonists after the War

Harald Mors

Following the Gran Sasso Operation, Mors remained as a General Staff officer of 2nd Division Fallschirmjäger until the end of January 1944. He was then transferred to the Russian front, never knowing if this was due to normal operational changes, or as a punishment for his demands to publish the official version of events during the Gran Sasso raid. In the final phase of the war he was appointed chief inspector of the official Goslar paratrooper school. In March 1945 he was a staff officer in 3rd Division Fallschirmjäger, part of Schlemm's First Army, and was deployed in the Ruhr region, where the attack of Crerar's 2nd Canadian Army and Dempsey's 2nd British Army was concentrated. The German troops were trapped in the Ruhr pocket and Mors was taken prisoner.

He had a brief respite in a prison camp, before being freed in September 1945. A report made on him by the Gestapo in 1938 had labelled him 'politically suspect', following an opinion he had expressed about Nazim. He now used this in his favour, and so a phrase that had caused him problems in his military career, now helped open the doors to freedom.

After the war, he worked as a dance teacher in Ulm. At the end of the 1950s, his help was requested in the creation of the army of the Federal German Republic (Bundeswehr). Thanks to his knowledge of languages, in 1956 he held various posts in NATO. He was promoted to colonel in 1961 and was sent to Madrid for his final posting. Despite 'sharing' the city with Otto Skorzeny, he never interacted with him, and on the contrary, tried to avoid his presence. As Nicolás Hoelscher recounts, they did meet at two official meetings, but Mors 'avoided speaking to him'. Regarding these meetings, Mors himself remembers, 'I had nothing to say to him and he had no explanation for me either. We both knew perfectly well how the events had unfolded at the Gran Sasso, as well as what our respective roles had been.'

He retired from active service in 1969, and lived in Berg, by Lake Starnberg, from 1964. He began to write his life story, but never spoke about the success of the Gran Sasso. Instead, he wrote down his family history in ten volumes, from the seventeenth century, until the dawn of the new millennium. However, he did write about his experiences at the Gran Sasso in a small work published in 1992.

He avoided interviews, being afraid of polemics and manipulations, saying that he didn't want politics to distort historical truth, as often happens. He died on 11 February 2001, at the age of 90.

Otto Skorzeny

Skorzeny's fame increased considerably after the day of Mussolini's liberation, and he became Hitler's trusted man for the most daring and dangerous missions, such as those that envisaged the capture of Marshal Pétain or the Yugoslavian Tito. These missions could not be completed, but for reasons that had nothing to do with the Austrian.

After having collaborated in the Stauffenberg plot to assassinate Hitler on 20 July 1944, in the autumn of that year he received orders to capture the Regent of Hungary, Admiral Miklós Horthy, who had been secretly negotiating an armistice with the Soviets. Leading a commando unit, Skorzeny stormed the Budapest castle and occupied it in a well-executed coup. Although Horthy had abandoned the residence a few moments before, the objective of the mission had been fulfilled: the government had fallen. Control of the country was now taken over by the pro-German Ferenc Szálasi, who would keep Hungary's interests tied to those of Germany until the end of the war.

Meanwhile, Skorzeny once again received Hitler's personal congratulations, and was awarded the German Cross in Gold and a promotion to lieutenant colonel. However, his main mission was carried out months later in the Ardennes, during the last big German offensive, which began in the early hours of the morning on 16 December.

Soon after the Allied invasion of Normandy (6 June 1944) Skorzeny began selecting and training an SS brigade that could speak perfect American-English. He acquired American uniforms, equipment and vehicles, thus giving life to the 'fantasy' 150th Brigade that operated behind enemy lines during Operation Greif. The unit was ordered to spread panic among the enemy: motorised troops on board jeeps had to swap and change road signs, replacing them with wrong ones; they had to cut telephone lines; mark nonexistent minefields and divert armoured columns coming from the American rear. In a second successive phase, the armoured brigade would then capture the bridges over the River Meuse.

The first part was carried out perfectly: almost every jeep unit came back to the German lines after having spread chaos among the Allies. After a series of setbacks, the second phase had to be cancelled. Despite this, the consequences of the Germans' raid while wearing American uniforms were enough to increase Skorzeny's fame, so that now more than ever he was considered, 'the most dangerous man in the world'.

Following the fall of the Third Reich and the defeat of Germany, SS-Standartenführer Skorzeny surrendered to the Americans in Baviera on 15 May 1945. Just two months earlier, on 8 March, he had been awarded his Oak Leaves to the Knight's Cross of the Iron Cross. However, as an American prisoner, he now had to face a judicial process. In September 1945 he was taken to Nuremberg, but his 'celebrity status' meant that he was besieged by journalists and photographers. Skorzeny was then transferred to Dachau and the trail began in July 1946. He was found not guilty of committing war crimes, but was not granted bail.

In 1948, Skorzeny escaped from his prison camp and all trace of him was quickly lost. In 1950 he fled to Spain thanks to the 'Nansen passport', which he was able to obtain due to his Austrian nationality and the condescending attitude of the Spanish government. Skorzeny worked as a mechanical engineer and had many contacts abroad. He had already established contacts with German businessmen and bankers during the Nuremberg trials, who after the war, had gone into the construction business. In 1952, his import and export company completed a large transaction between Spain and Germany to supply railway equipment and various machinery.

Meanwhile, the courts had rendered a positive sentence about his de-Nazification, and Skorzeny was now regarded as a 'respectable businessman'. He even worked as a war correspondent for German newspapers. Nicolás Hoelscher, a former German paratrooper now settled in Madrid, remembers:

> For some time he called himself Rolf Steinbauer, and he lived in Madrid, near my house (in the López de Hoyos area). When we met he began to boast about his adventures during the war, I interrupted him and asked directly, 'Otto, why don't you tell us the real role you played in the liberation of Mussolini?'

The aura of an adventurer that surrounded Skorzeny led many to believe that he was behind a plan, commissioned by the Arab League, to kidnap the deposed Sultan of Morocco. He also became the man who had supposedly collaborated with the Israeli Secret Service

(Mosad) in 1963 to convince a team of Austrian and German technicians working in Egypt on the *Al Zafir* programme to abandon the project, which involved the construction of surface-to-air missiles that the Egyptian government would have used against Israel. The so-called Operation Domocles underwent a radical change when the head of Egyptian Intelligence, Mahmud Khalil, revealed that *Al Zafir* was, to a large extent, a decoy. Yet another story among the many dark sides of the Skorzeny legend.

It is difficult to imagine a man such as him, who loved to 'live dangerously', completely adapting to the smooth rhythms of daily life, without any adventures. For most people he was the 'Liberator of Mussolini', but if the legend speaks of Skorzeny, then history holds another story entirely. During the post-war period, Student never stopped pressurising the Austrian, even revealing that he had a document signed by Skorzeny in which he had written: 'I have never stated that I was the liberator of Mussolini. It was always others who affirmed this'. He simply said that he had never not been [the one to free Mussollini]. Skorzeny died in Madrid on 5 July 1975, and was buried in Döbling cemetery, Vienna.

Bibliography

Books

AA.VV, *Erinnerungen aus Weltkrieg II. Nachrichtenzug im Fallschirmjäger Lehr-Batl./Rg. Herrmann*, Self-published, 1986.

Bosshammer Bernhard and Bliss, Heinz, *Das Fallschirmjäger-Lehr-Regiment*, Druckerei Köhler, Witzenhausen 1992.

Bosshammer, Bernhard and Bliss, Heinz, *Sturm auf den Gran Sasso. Der kühne Handstreich zur Befreiung Mussolinis durch das Fallschirmjäger-Lehr-Battaillon*, Druckerei Köhler, Witzenhausen 1990.

Busch, Erich, *Die Fallschirmjäger-Chronik 1935-1945*, Podzun-Pallas Verlag, Friedberg 1983.

Chazette, A, *Fallschirmjäger. Les parachutistes allemands en France 1943-1944*, Histoire et Fortifications, Paris.

Centro Turistico Aquiliano, *Atti del convengo storico: Il Gran Sasso e Mussolini 1943-1993*, 1993.

Forczyk, Robert, *Rescuing Mussolini. Gran Sasso 1943*, Osprey, Oxford 2010.

Patricelli, Marco, *Liberate il Duce. Gran Sasso 1943: la vera storia dell'operazione Quercia*, Mondadori, Milano 2002.

Patricelli, Marco, *Operazione Quercia. Liberate Mussolini!*, Solfanell, Chieti 1993.

Petacco, Arrigo and Zavoli, Sergio, *Dal Gran Consiglio al Gran Sasso: Una storia da rifare*, Rizzoli, Milano 1973.

Petacco, Arrigo, *La Seconda Guerra Mondiale*, Armando Curcio Editore, Roma 1978.

Radl, Karl, *Die Blitzbefreiung Mussolinis. Mit Skorzeny am Gran Sasso*, Pour Le Mérite, Kiel 1996.

Salas Larrazábal, Jesús, *Guernica: el bombardeo*, Madrid 1981.

Schröder, J., *Italiens Kriegsaustritt 1943*, Musterschmidt Verlag, Göttingen 1969.

Skorzeny, Otto, *Vive peligrosamente*, Acervo, Barcelona 1965.

Solar, David, *La caída de los dioses*, La Esfera de los Libros, Madrid 2006.

Stimpel, H., *Die deutsche Fallschirmtruppe 1942-1945. Einsätze auf Kriegsschauplätzen im Süden*, Mittler, Hamburg 1998.

Articles

Bliss, Heinz, *Der Sturm auf den Gran Sasso durch das Fallschirmjäger-Lehrbataillon*, in 'Der Deutsche Fallschirmjäger', July/August 2003.

Bosshammer, B. and Kittel W., *Die Befreiung Mussolinis auf dem Gran Sasso am 12. 9. 1943*, in and 'Treue Kameraden. Zeitschrift des Bayersichen Soldatenbundes' 1974 E.V Nr. 5, September/October 2003.

Gerlach, Hans, *Bravourstreich im Hochgebirge*, in 'Der Deutsche Fallschirmjäger', 9 September 1953.

Gerlach, Hans, *In Sturzflug über den Abgrund*, in Bosshammer, Bernhard and Bliss, Heinz, 'Das Fallschirmjäger-Lehr-Regiment', Druckerei Köhler, Witzenhausen 1992.

Kurth, Joachim, *Misión especial*, in 'Revista de Aeronáutica' n° 135, 1952.

Langguth, Gerhard, *Stellungnahme Gran Sasso Nr. 1/97 DDF* in '*Der Deutsche Fallschirmjäger*' n° 2, 1997.

Meyer-Wehner, Elimar, *Flug zum Gran Sasso*, in 'Der Deutsche Fallschirmjäger', 9 September 1953.

Schröder, Josef, *Skorzeny gefährdete die Aktion*, in '*Zeitungen als Dokumente*' n° 9, Orbis, Hamburg.

Solar, David, *Operación en el Gran Sasso: Duce, sois libre*, in 'La Aventura de la Historia' n° 60, October 2003.

Student Kurt, *Auch ohne Skorzeny und die SS wäre die Aktion gelungen* in 'Zeitungen als Dokumente' n° 9, Orbis, Hamburg.

Thorwald, Jürgen, *Was Skorzeny nicht berichtet...* in 'REVUE. Die Weltillustrierte', N° 18, München, 6 May 1950.